TENNIS

WHAT REALLY MATTERS

GUNDARS TILMANIS

Tilmanis Tennis
Portland, Oregon

TESTIMONIALS FOR

TENNIS: WHAT REALLY MATTERS

"So much of this game is common sense. Til has put it well and his advice is sound.

– Arthur R. Ashe, Jr.

"Gundars Tilmanis Is a real "pro". His book is as enjoyable to read as his on-court presentations are to watch."

– Jack Kramer

"Til is internationally recognized as a coach and teacher. His ability to creatively combine tennis information and entertainment is unmatched."

– James E. Loehr, EdD. Sports Psychologist

"I have met and heard all the "big names" in the tennis business. Til is by far the best communicator. He presents information the way the average person can understand."

– Brett Hall Tennis Professional USPTA

Tilmanis Tennis/Tennis: What Really Matters
Printed in the United States of America

Tennis: What Really Matters/ Gundars Tilmanis -- 1st ed.

ISBN 9798869606310 Print Edition

Content

1: Minimizing Your Mistakes 1

2: Putting Your Opponent in A Position To Make Mistakes 17

3: Singles Tips: Things That Matter and Will Make A Difference 35

4: Observations on Match Play 59

5: Playing Smart Doubles 71

6: The Mental Game - Keep Your Head Don't Lose It 89

7: Off Court Tips That Can Help Improve on Court Performance 111

8: Warm Up and Physical Fitness 119

9: Til Tennis Stories...149

I'd like to thank Kathleen Bergquist for her help in transcribing my collection of handwritten notes into a legible and usable format. Kathleen has worked with me on my books in the past and I appreciate her willingness to indulge my thought process!

Chapter 1

Minimizing Your Mistakes

INTRODUCTION

In 2015, I can remember reading an article in The Oregonian newspaper. The University of Oregon baseball coach, Coach Horton, was asked a question. "How come your team is in a slump?" His answer: "We have to cut down on our mistakes and force our opponents to make mistakes." And I thought to myself, *That's what we should be trying to do to win a tennis match!*

Let's talk about how we, as coaches, can help our players minimize their mistakes.

One: We have to explain to our students that there are two barriers that they must keep in mind when stroking the ball.

FIRST BARRIER – THE NET

The net is 3 feet high at midcourt and 3 feet 6 inches at the sidelines. Major Walter Wingfield, an Englishman, was responsible for these net dimensions. He published the first book of rules for tennis in 1874.

If he had suggested a net height of 2 feet 6 inches at midcourt, that would have made players much happier.

Regardless, to hit the ball over the first barrier (the net), a player should picture "lifting the ball over the net."

When hitting a forehand drive, players may have a looped or straight backswing as long as the racquet head ends up behind and below the ball contact point.

For young beginners, the key checkpoints for the racquet backswing are to pretend they are shaking hands with a dwarf, contact the ball out in front, brush the racquet "uphill" to shake hands with a giant, fan across the body to finish the shot with the racquet over the left shoulder. In other words, an uphill brush, a fan across in front of your face, and ending up to "hook" the racquet over the left shoulder.

Picture a "brush," "fan," and "hook" racquet path. It helps to have the players picture the path of the ball flight over the net and not zipping the ball in a "flat" trajectory, barely passing over the top of the net—that would be a low percentage shot.

The path of the ball flight would be more accurately pictured as a side view of a whale hump or a rainbow or a side view of Coach Til sleeping on his back.

SECOND BARRIER – COURT DIMENSIONS

The ball must be controlled to land inside the court dimensions. Ball control really means racquet control. Choking up on the racquet handle will help give players more control. Swinging the racquet at "medium" speed will increase ball control. The racquet imparting "spin" to the ball will increase ball control.

Once your students have developed strokes within the range of correctness, emphasize not getting hung up on technique or looking good. Have students focus on hitting the ball over the net and in the court.

I like to ask my students a question: "Where do your groundstrokes finish?" The racquet ends up over the left shoulder on the forehand and over the right shoulder on the backhand. Yes, that's where the racquet finishes. But the stroke finishes where the ball lands. Be happy if the ball lands where you have "aimed."

Have a target area in mind when stroking the ball. That will give your stroke more purpose.

Focus on "over the net and in the court."

TWO: PLAYERS DO THREE THINGS OVER AND OVER HUNDREDS OF TIMES IN A MATCH--ORGANIZE, PLACE, RECOVER.

Organize. Set up as comfortably as you can before the time to hit. As you are getting set up with footwork and racquet preparation, you should ask yourself the question: "To hit or not to hit?" Someone a long time ago asked a similar question. If comfortable, hit aggressively with recommended form. If uncomfortable, off balance, or out of position, then improvise.

Place. Place the ball in a strategically smart place. If in trouble, hit deep down the middle or short sliders off to the sides. If comfortable, hit to the opponent's weak side, open court, or with an aggressive pattern of play.

Recover. Just as quickly as you move off to hit a shot, recover to either home base or a strategically smart court position. You must assume your opponent will get the ball back.

Make good decisions by practicing "organizing, placing, recovering." Groove the moves using smart drills.

THREE: GET COMFORTABLE AND SPEND ENOUGH TIME ON EACH SHOT.

When you are hitting a shot, you are executing a skill. Work hard to get comfortable, in balance with the ball a comfortable distance away. Head steady, eyes wide open, stare at the ball. Spend enough time on each shot if you can.

If you rush your shot or hit half a shot and make an error, where are you running to? Nowhere! The point is over.

Remember, you are the carrier of the racquet. Hustle to get to the ball so the racquet can do its job. If you don't get to the ball in time to hit a technically solid shot, you owe your racquet an apology. *Sorry I didn't get you over to the ball in time. I promise I will hustle better next time.*

Be extra alert if the ball is landing close to the lines. Open your eyes wide so you can make the right call. Remember, you can return a shot and immediately call "out" if, in fact, it actually was!

FOUR: CATCH THE BALL WITH SPIN.

When we talk about ball control, we really mean racquet control.

If you hit the ball too flat, it will take off, and who knows where it will go, but who doesn't care, in fact, who hates tennis, and who loves baseball. In fact, "Who's on first, what's on second, and I don't know is on third." (Taken from a legendary baseball skit by Abbot and Costello in the 1950s called "Who's on First!?")

Grab the ball with spin. Most coaches, including Til, tell their students to topspin when they can (the most aggressive hitting) and to slice when they have to or, because of a strategy, want to.

Topspin. To get topspin on your groundstrokes, brush up the back of the ball, fan your racquet across in front of your body, and hook the racquet over your shoulder for the follow through. The racquet face can stay "open" at ball contact as long as the racquet face is swung "uphill" from below the ball contact point to above the ball contact point (swing from low to high).

Brushing the back of the ball from low to high will impart topspin to the ball.

Slice. Hitting your groundstrokes with a slice. Open the racquet face and "slide" your racquet under the ball. "Cup" your racquet under the ball (swing from high to low).

Slicing the Ball Deep	Slicing the Ball Short
Swing aggressively: much racquet head speed	**Swing** less vigorously: less racquet head speed
Follow Through: long follow through	**Follow Through**: short follow through
Direction of Swing: horizontal	**Direction of Swing**: starts horizontal then drops down vertically
Type of Shot: more of a power shot	**Type of Shot**: more of a "feel" shot

Blend the racquet head speed, the length of the swing, and the trajectory of the racquet head to get the desired result.

Volleys. Hitting volleys too "flat" will send the ball off the strings with a lot of pace but with little control. By hitting volleys too flat, who knows where the ball will go?

Volleying with a little slice, by cupping the racquet under the ball, will grab the ball for a minute fraction of a second and give the stroke more control.

Serving (Slice or Kick). Hitting with a little spin technique to supplement the power element will help increase consistency. An effective serve is a blend of speed and spin.

A first serve is hit with a high level of racquet head speed with a little spin. A second serve is generally hit with a slightly lower racquet head speed and a little more spin.

To emphasize this blend of speed and spin, I ask my students a question: "Would you rather hit two aces in a match or get 85 percent of your first serves in?" Hopefully, they will answer with 85 percent of first services in!

Drop shots. To hit effectively, drop shots are a "touch" shot hit with an abundance of slice. Think of a drop shot as being a volley that "went wrong," the same short, open face backswing, but instead of aggressively attacking the ball, hit the ball with a looser grip and more of a "caressing" action (extra slice). Pretend you are picking up an injured bird.

FIVE: BE CONSISTENT.

Have a "mindset" to keep the ball going. If you hit five to six balls over in a row, before you have to do anything, your opponent will error. Put your ego that says I'm going to hit a lot of quick winners in your pocket. Put your jacket on the bench and be prepared to rally for a while.

THREE TRUE STORIES

Betty Harless

Betty was a regular student of mine for many years, taking private lessons, group lessons, and tennis camps. She approached me one day and asked me a question: "I have taken in so much information from you on improving my tennis that I feel overloaded with instruction. In a nutshell, what should I be focusing on?"

I replied, "Betty, this is true for both singles and doubles. Keep the ball going and wait for a mistake from your opponent or an opportunity for you to finish the point. Period." We coaches have to make up a lot of other stuff to make a living.

Bob Thompson

Bob was a member of my seniors' tennis team. Following a match, sitting around chatting, I asked him if he played college tennis. He replied, "Yes! I played #1 for the University of Seattle. The #2 player challenged me three times during our four years of competition, and he never could beat me." That was a very dominating statement, I thought. "What do you mean?" I asked. He replied, "Well, he would make a mistake after three hits, and I would make a mistake after six hits. So, if you did the math, I would never lose to that guy!"

Cynthia Cyler

Cynthia was a college player who struggled to maintain consistency, i.e., hitting a couple of balls in the court, then hitting the wall, the lights, or the net. In short, she was self-destructing. So, my job was to help her sustain a lengthier rally.

I called Cynthia to the net and told her we would play a game. I went over the rules. I told Cynthia that I would feed her easy, comfortable groundstrokes if she hit two in a row over the net and got the shot in. Then she'd get a point. If she missed the first or second shot I fed her, then I would win the point. We would play whoever got to 11 points first. "I got it, Coach," she said and smiled, thinking she would win.

We played, and I beat her 11-3. She couldn't do it—get two balls in a row consistently over the net and into the court. Do you know what she said? She wanted to do it again. I beat her again 11-7. After a couple more games, she was beating me. She got the message! And then she started having more match successes by keeping the ball going.

SIX: STAY WITH YOUR GAME PLAN OF CONTROLLED AGGRESSIVENESS.

Hazel Wightman

Hazel won the US Open Women's Singles titles in 1909, 1910 and 1911. At that high level of competition, she had a "golden match," winning a match without losing a point.

After retirement, Hazel taught tennis in Boston, Massachusetts. Her trademark words of wisdom were:

"If you don't miss, you will win."

"If you don't miss, and you can place the ball where you want, I will come and watch you play."

"If you don't miss, and you can place the ball where you want and hit the ball hard, I will be happy to buy a ticket to watch you play."

Her message was:

1. Be consistent.
2. Move the ball around the court.
3. Finish points.

Hers was a consistency to aggressiveness theme or controlled aggressiveness.

Bill Tilden

Bill Tilden ruled the tennis world in the 1920s, not losing a match of any consequence for about ten years. A reporter asked, "How come you are so good?" After a short time to reflect, he replied, "I have a defensive mind and aggressive strokes."

His was a great blend of controlled aggressiveness.

Jack Kramer

I was fortunate to have spent time with Jack Kramer as a co-speaker at a number of tennis coaches workshops. Jack ruled the tennis world in the late 1940s and early 1950s. He was the father of the aggressive serve and volley and finishing points with a winning shot game.

I asked Jack about his recipe for winning. He said it was controlled power. I read that the same way as controlled aggressiveness.

SEVEN: MIMIC THE TOP PLAYERS IN THE WORLD.

The top-ranked players in the world today have a very similar game plan. They are "grinders," hitting their shots with consistency and as high a rallying speed as they can. They wait for a mistake from their opponent or an opportunity to aggressively finish the point themselves by becoming stroke makers.

The key to their high ranking is the game plan of controlled aggressiveness. Patiently grinding, under control, with their personal rally speed, patterns of play, earning mistakes, or opportunities to become an aggressive stroke maker.

When watching today's top players, one cannot help but notice a dramatic "speed-up" of player movement and their rallying speed. Some contributing factors to this include:

- Racquet technology
- Training methods
- Coaching methods
- Stroke techniques
- Health and dietary habits
- Physical fitness

EIGHT: HAVE THE RIGHT MINDSET WHEN SERVING AND RECEIVING SERVE.

The mind sets the body in motion. Otherwise, the body will just go through the motions.

When serving a first serve, think, *Destroy. This ball is not coming back.*

When serving a second serve, think, *I will hurt them so badly, I'll get a garbage ball return.*

When receiving a first serve, think, *Get the ball back in play, deep down the middle, the server has the advantage.*

When receiving a second serve, think, *Smile, move up a little, focus on hitting a more aggressive shot.*

Mix up your serves so you are not too predictable, both the type of serve and the placement.

SERVING TO THE AD COURT

Work on serving immediately to a right-hander's backhand. Take a more sideways stance, ball lift a little more over your head, and swing the racquet more to the right. Picture the ball as a clock face; swing or fan the racquet head from 7 o'clock to 2 o'clock, then wrist or hook the racquet face over the ball to fire it down into the court to a right-hander's backhand.

PULLING YOUR OPPONENT OFF THE COURT WITH YOUR SERVE

When Serving to the Deuce Side

A slightly more open stance, ball lift a little more to the right and a shade more in front. Think of a combination of slice and topspin since the ball is traveling across the high part of the net. Cross the singles sideline.

When Serving to the Ad Side (similar to serving to a right-hander's backhand) A more closed stance, a little more sideways. Lift the ball a little more overhead, swing up the back of the ball, and follow through a little more to the right (kick serve). Cross the singles sideline. Serve from various spots along the baseline to force the receiver to adjust. Practice serving into the receiver's body, forcing an uncomfortable, off-balance return.

When Returning to a Serve and Volleyer

Mix up hitting down the line with speed, hitting a speed ball at them, or a soft angle cross court. Don't always try to immediately pass the approaching server; mix up dropping the return at the server's feet and then hitting out on a passing shot from their first volley or half volley.

NINE: PICK A TARGET FOR YOUR SHOTS.

Picking a target area for your strokes will give your shots more purpose.

For example: When receiving a red-light ball (a tough, difficult shot), place your return somewhere you cannot get hurt too badly, i.e., hit the ball deep down the middle of the court or sliced low and off to the sides.

For example: When receiving a wide, difficult ball to your backhand side, return the ball with a crosscourt slice, either deep or short and angled. That will give your opponent a difficult shot and allow you to just take a few recovery movements to be in the middle of the angle of possible return.

For example: When receiving a wide, difficult ball to your forehand side, return the ball with a high arcing topspin drive cross court. This will allow you extra time to recover and take just a few steps to be in the middle of the angle of possible return.

When you are pulled wide and feel like you are off the court and out of position, the best shot selection is to hit a winning shot down the line or a high, deep lob that will give you time to recover.

For example: When chasing a short, low-bouncing wide ball that is close to the net, choose a smart target. Pushing the ball deep down the middle of the court will not work out well for you. Your opponent can hit an open court winner. Your best target is a shot deep down the line. Your opponent will be forced to hit a tough passing shot, and you have 2-3 steps to position yourself in the middle of the angle of possible return. Another good target would be to hit a sharply-angled cross-court slice shot for a winner.

Here's your mindset and shot selection for putting away easy, green-light balls. You don't have to break the ball to win the point.

Remember that speed all by itself is useless.

Put a little something on the end of speed.
- Speed with control
- Speed with placement
- Speed with feeling

Be mindful when angle without speed is going to win for you. For example, angling off an easy volley that lands in the service box and immediately cuts the sidelines is where you don't need a lot of speed. However, when hitting a deep angle shot into the deep corner, you do need more speed.

Angle and speed don't usually mix very well. It's like dripping lemon juice into milk. It can be an ugly mix.

If your put away shot had two targets, one the size of an elephant (open court shot) and the other the size of a flea (hitting behind your opponent), which target would you aim for? I would aim for the flea and hit it right between the eyes! No, you wouldn't! You'd aim for the bigger target. Occasionally, hit a backfoot shot behind your opponent. Never backfoot a player that is too wide off the court, tired, or over 40; they will give up and not recover.

TEN: BE PHYSICALLY FIT.

A serious competitive player has to be competent in four areas.

1. Have sound strokes within the range of recommended mechanics. They are the tools that do the work.

2. Have smart strategies to make life miserable for your opponents.

3. Be mentally tough to stay on track and make smart decision.

4. Be physically fit so you are able to compete for the duration of the match.

THE IMPORTANCE OF BEING IN GREAT PHYSICAL CONDITION

Remember you, as we said before, are the carrier of the racquet. Hustle to get to the ball so the racquet can do its job. If you don't get to the ball in time to hit a technically solid shot, you owe your racquet an apology. "Sorry I didn't get you over to the ball in time. I promise I will hustle better next time."

You have a terrific advantage if you can set up for your shots in the deciding set just as well as you did in the first game of the first set.

A physically fit player can always set up well before hitting a shot. They will not have to improvise as much and will make fewer errors. However, if you are physically exhausted during the closing stages of a tough match, do a couple of things:

1. Take the allotted time between points and changeovers to rest.

2. Take some calculated, smart risks to shorten the rallies by opportunistically coming to the net or pulling your opponent to the net.

3. At changeovers, take the time to hydrate and upgrade your energy food intake.

Take the time to work in physical fitness and conditioning so you can sustain your game plan of controlled aggressiveness for the entirety of your matches.

ELEVEN: MAKE SURE YOUR GAME PLAN MATCHES YOUR ABILITY.

Select a game plan and strategy that matches your physical and mental makeup, tennis-playing experience, and age.

For example, it is difficult for a short, not very experienced, not very mobile, volley hater to have a net-rushing strategy. As a developing player, play with your rally speed. Don't emulate a top player's rally speed that you just watched on TV. Their rally speed is much faster than yours. Your rally speed will go up as you physically and mentally develop and stockpile more experiences.

Use patterns of play that you feel comfortable with. Stockpile other patterns of play that would be effective when playing certain types of opponents. For example, a pusher, a slow mover, a slugger, a constant net rusher, or a player that has an extremely powerful forehand.

TWELVE: BE MENTALLY TOUGH.

If you mess up a shot, don't think of it as a mistake. Think of it as a bad decision and analyze what stroke or strategy changes you'd make that would be a better choice next time.

Analyzing what happened:

1. Did my opponent hit too good a shot?
2. Did I rush my shot?
3. Did I try to hit the ball too hard?
4. Did I choose the wrong shot?
5. Did I use the wrong technique?

The ball that approaches in a trajectory that is between a high volley or a low overhead is often missed. Use an adjusted technique overhead (a slow controlled wrist action or a "pop" block shot). It's a mistake to choose to hit an overhead that's too aggressive. You should not make up a shot that's not there.

The ball that approaches and is very low and close to the net is often missed. It is not an opportunity for an aggressive shot. It needs a hang-in-there technique, a push or roll deep down the line, or a sharply-sliced angle cross court shot.

Chapter 2

Putting Your Opponent in a Position to Make Mistakes

ONE: STUDY YOUR OPPONENT:

WHAT STYLE OF PLAYER IS COMING AT YOU?

Does your opponent have a weak side?
   a. Watch the technique
   b. Watch the dynamics of the approaching ball

Take advantage of knowing the weaker side. Be careful, however, to not overplay your opponent's weaker side. It's possible their weakness could become a strength.

Analyze your own weaknesses to figure out what you have to work on by asking yourself this question: "What would my game plan be if I played against myself?" It would be close. In the end, I think you would win.

TWO: START THE MATCH WITH YOUR FAVORITE PATTERNS OF PLAY.

You will feel more comfortable and confident. Then select some patterns of play and strategies of play that your opponent would struggle with.

PATTERNS OF PLAY AGAINST CERTAIN OTHER PLAYING STYLES

a) A good hitter but a slow mover

1. Make them move corner to corner and occasionally backfoot.

2. Two or three deep drives followed by a short angled slider (in short, make them move).

b) A slugger, a player hitting too aggressively (love playing an opponent that gives you points)

1. Make them hit a lot of balls.

2. Mix up your shots to force them to hit uncomfortably but aggressively. High, deep topspin drives, pulling them wide, dropping the ball short.

c) An opponent with an amazing forehand

1. Pull them wide on their forehand side to open up their backhand as a target.

2. Hit uncomfortable balls for them to handle like high, wide, short (so they have trouble being aggressive with their forehand).

d) A compulsive net rusher

1. Hit them deep, high-bouncing, topspin drives to force them to back up and hit under pressure.

2. You could approach the net at opportune times, forcing them to hit passing shots (which may not be their preferred rally situation).

3. As the opponent approaches the net, occasionally drop the ball low at their feet to force a pop-up, then go all out for a passing shot.

4. As the opponent approaches the net, be mindful of your passing shot targets.

5. Down the line is a speed ball shot, the target being a long rectangle. The cross court target area is more of a soft placement shot, a closer to the net triangle area. Once you have hit a couple of passing drives, a lob is a good choice.

e) A pusher

For how to beat a pusher, refer to the chapter on the Mental Game and read the section "Some thoughts on handling specific adversities."

THREE: ANALYZE THE ONCOMING BALL AND ASK YOURSELF WHETHER TO HIT OR NOT TO HIT.

If on balance and comfortable, hit a regular aggressive shot. If off balance, uncomfortable, or out of position, improvise. Once you have a so-called recommended shot down, work on techniques of improvisation.

I first realized the importance of teaching improvisation in 1977 while watching USC's Men's Tennis Coach, George Toley, give a presentation at the USTA's National Tennis Coaches Conference in New York. George, demonstrating on court, fed a student at the net a wide, fast-approaching ball. The student contacted the ball late, behind his body, and volleyed the ball into the crowd. George's analysis was that the student tried to get too comfortable and did not have the time to set up to hit a classic volley. Improvise, he said, just get the racquet to a position for a clean contact. Forget about body preparation and looking good. It was an eye-opening moment for me. I left the lecture, went upstairs to my hotel room, and wrote for two and a half hours on my thoughts about stroke improvisation teaching.

Singles Game Plan Flow Chart

Gundars Tilmanis

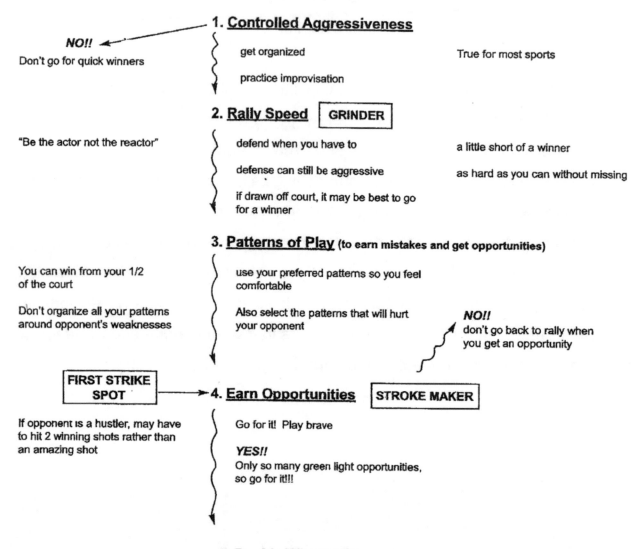

1. Controlled Aggressiveness

NO!!
Don't go for quick winners

get organized

practice improvisation

True for most sports

2. Rally Speed   GRINDER

"Be the actor not the reactor"

defend when you have to

defense can still be aggressive

if drawn off court, it may be best to go
for a winner

a little short of a winner

as hard as you can without missing

3. Patterns of Play (to earn mistakes and get opportunities)

You can win from your 1/2
of the court

Don't organize all your patterns
around opponent's weaknesses

use your preferred patterns so you feel
comfortable

Also select the patterns that will hurt
your opponent

NO!!
don't go back to rally when
you get an opportunity

FIRST STRIKE
SPOT   ➔   **4. Earn Opportunities**   STROKE MAKER

If opponent is a hustler, may have
to hit 2 winning shots rather than
an amazing shot

Go for it! Play brave

YES!!
Only so many green light opportunities,
so go for it!!!

5. Decide What to Do

a) winner

- speed and angle to the deep
  corners
- open court
- drop shot option
- do not need a great shot if
  opponent is off court

b) open court shot

- crosscourt go with angle
- down the line go with speed
- back foot
- no back foot if opponent is
  pulled extremely wide

c) approach shot

- to weak side
- to open court
- down the line
- approach down middle
- approach deep, volley
  angle

As players move down the flow chart from 1→2→3→4, they are hitting with their rally speed (a nice blend of speed and control). At level 5, a player becomes a more aggressive stroke maker with an opportunity to finish the point.

Important: I have my students study and understand the Singles Game Plan Flow Chart. I spend time discussing with them which parts of the chart they need to work on.

For example: A student trying to hit a winning shot each time they hit the ball should focus on hitting with their rally speed.

For example: A student earning an opportunity to aggressively finish the point but chooses to passively rally the ball back to their opponent.

For example: A player needing to expand their patterns of play.

Let's take a closer look at the Singles Game Plan Flow Chart. The overall umbrella of the game plan is called Controlled Aggressiveness:

1. Controlled aggressiveness. True for most sports---basketball, volleyball, soccer, lacrosse, water polo, and shopping. The key ingredient is consistency. Keeping the ball going under control, waiting for a mistake or an opportunity to be aggressive.
2. Rally speed. The first thing to do is keep the ball going with your rally speed by hitting as hard as you can without missing and hitting a little short of a winner.
3. Patterns of play. Develop patterns of play that will force your opponent to make mistakes or give you an easy ball you can take advantage of.

Examples include:

a. Corner to corner and occasionally hit behind your opponent to catch them recovering to the middle.

b. Two deep balls followed by a short angled slice.

c. Hit all drives cross court for a while.

d. Mostly drive, occasionally hit some high-bouncing topspin drives, occasionally some short slices.

4. Earn opportunities. You will earn opportunities to finish the point. This is called the first strike spot.

5. Decide what to do.

a. Hit a winner. When receiving a short, easy ball, hit aggressively into the deep corners or hit a drop shot. Remember, speed all by itself is useless, so add a little something on the end of speed. Speed and angle, placement, control, or feeling.

b. Open court shot. Pull your opponent wide and off the court to give yourself an open court shot.

   i. If cross court is open, go with more of an angle shot and cut the sideline.

   ii. If down the line is open, hit with speed and depth.

   iii. Third choice is to backfoot, hit behind your opponent as they are recovering quickly to midcourt. Don't backfoot an opponent who is tired or over 40 because they will give up and not recover.

c. An approach shot. If the opponent's shot is a low-bouncing ball close to the net or a short ball a little deeper than midcourt, hit an approach shot, a little short of a winner. You have decided to hurt your opponent, not kill them, and finish the point with a volley or overhead. Be a grinder with your rally speed and use some patterns of play to earn one of the three easy ball situations. Finish the point by being a stroke maker.

As you move down the flow chart from 1→2→3→4, you have a good chance to win the point with your consistency and smart patterns of play. Supplement this defensive play with offensive play when one of the easy ball situations arises, like a short easy ball, an open court shot, or an approach shot at level 5.

A player able to win points in both defensive and offensive situations will be asking their parents to build them a trophy cupboard.

Hit the ball with as high a rally speed as you can:

A little short of a winner and as hard as you can without missing.

Students should not emulate the rally speed of their idol star tennis player. Their speed will naturally increase as they physically mature and gain more playing experience.

The player with the highest rally speed has the best chance of winning a match.

BE DESPERATE TO KEEP THE BALL GOING.

I tell my players if you can get 5-6 balls over in a row before you have to do anything, your opponent will mess up. Put your ego, which wants you to hit a lot of quick winners, in your pocket.

As mentioned in the previous chapter, I repeat because it is important.

The top ranked players in the world today have very similar game plans. They are grinders hitting their shots with consistency and as high rally speed as they can.

They wait for a mistake from their opponent or an opportunity to aggressively finish the point themselves by becoming stroke makers.

The key to their high ranking is their game plan of controlled aggressiveness.

FIVE: IF YOU ARE TOO PREDICTABLE, YOU ARE TOO PREDICTABLE.

Give your opponent your normal playing style, then mix it up with your rallying, particularly if you are losing 90% of the baseline rallies.

Occasionally:

1. Hit deep topspin drives.
2. Shortish wide slices (particularly from your backhand to their backhand).
3. Rush the net at opportune times.
4. Occasionally serve and volley.
5. Drop shot to pull opponent to the net.

SIX: SHOT PLACEMENT

It is more important to hit your shots deep or angled than to rely on power.

A visual on ball placement:

- Pretend your opponent's court is in the shape of a donut.
  - ◊ Deep in front of the baseline
  - ◊ Wide close to the sidelines
  - ◊ Short close to the net
- Land the ball on the donut, not in the donut hole. That would give your opponent an easy ball, a cupcake, and you will spend a lot of time saying "good shot" and nodding your head. You will get a stiff neck to go with your sore and stiff elbow!

SEVEN: THREE BALL SPEEDS – THREE TRAFFIC LIGHTS

This is a concept that will help players understand the relationships between shot selection, improvisation, and anticipation. Players will develop a very valuable asset called a "game sense."

READ ON:

The ball enters your court with three possible speeds:

1. A comfortable, rallying ball speed

2. A fast, high, wide, tough to handle ball

3. An easy ball, no problem, no pressure, chance to be aggressive ball speed

'

C'MON GREEN ! C'MON ! #*&+^#!~!#*!

To help a player visualize the right reaction and subsequent strategy to match up with the incoming ball, link up the three incoming speeds with the three traffic lights:

1. Yellow: approaching ball, a comfortable rally ball
2. Red: a fast, high, wide, tough to handle ball
3. Green: an easy ball, no problem, first strike opportunity

Pay attention to the color of the ball coming at you. What color is coming at you most often? Yellow – yes! Take care of the red with a hang-in-there shot, defense, improvise, or if totally difficult, try for a winning shot if taken way off court.

Look forward to the green, be aggressive, go for it.

When receiving a first serve, the ball color is usually red. If your opponent misses the first serve, the second serve will usually be a yellow or green ball.

If you hit a great passing shot, expect to get a yellow or green ball.

If you hit a short lob, expect your opponent to give you a red ball.

One way of looking at your purpose when rallying is to get as many mistakes and green light balls as you can.

Smart patterns of play will reward you with green balls from your opponent. When you get a green ball, remember you don't have to break the ball to win the point.

Remember to make a wise choice and decide what is best to do for a winner, an open court shot, an approach shot, or a drop shot.

If the court is really wide open, remember that you don't need an elephant gun to kill a squirrel. You can hit a safer shot.

The following is so important that I'm going to repeat myself. Remember, speed all by itself is useless. Put something on the end of speed.

- Speed and feeling
- Speed and control
- Speed and placement

A recognition of the color of the incoming ball will help you make good decisions, particularly for shot selection and the recovery to a tactically smart court position so that you can continue to play with controlled aggression.

EIGHT: SMART CHOICE: A WINNER OR AN APPROACH

Hit an approach shot if you feel like you cannot effectively hit a winner. An approach shot is a little short of a winner. You have decided to hurt, not kill your opponent. And finish with a volley or an overhead.

Most coaches, including Til, teach to hit an approach shot to the open court or the weak side. Another target is to approach down the middle of the court— catching your opponent by surprise. This also takes away their ability to hit great angles.

Important! Three things have to take place to give you the best chance of winning the approach shot choice:

1. Come in on the right, easy midcourt ball.
2. Hurt them with the approach shot.
3. Follow the middle of the angle and split step as the opponent is about to hit the ball.

You may approach following a lob over the opponent's head, drive a volley or a second serve return. When receiving a short, wide ball, approach down the line (tactically a wiser shot). You will only need two steps to set up in the middle of the angle.

Use a variety of shots to approach, speed, topspin, sidespin slice (to keep the ball low) to throw off your opponent.

NINE: CUTTING THE SIDELINES

If all your shots are bisecting the baseline, you are not moving your opponent enough. Look for opportunities to cut the sidelines (that will pull your opponent off the court).

You will have three chances to win the point:
1. They don't get to the ball.
2. They get to the ball but mess up.
3. They struggle to get the ball back, giving you an open court shot or backfoot.

The sidelines open up when you get a wide easy ball at the baseline or get a short easy ball by the net.

It helps to be able to move your opponent wide off the court with your serve.

TEN: SMART SERVING

Since you can hurt your opponent more with your first serve, get a high percentage of first serves in rather than going for too many aces.

Blend speed, spin, and placement.

Work on moving your opponent off the court.

    a) Right-hander: Slice to the deuce side and kick to the ad side.

    b) Left-hander: Kick to the deuce side and slice to the ad side.

Change your serving position along the baseline (feel comfortable serving immediately to the backhand side).

A righthand serving to another right-hander:

    a) Backfoot behind

    b) Ball lift over head

    c) Swing to right

Serving into the body can be effective.

ELEVEN: IF YOUR OPPONENT IS A HUSTLER:

You may have to hit two winners to win the point rather than take a risky choice or ripping an amazing winner.

Always follow a put away shot by moving a little closer to the net in case your opponent struggles and gets the ball back.

TWELVE: WORK ON DEVELOPING BOTH DEFENSIVE AND OFFENSIVE SKILLS.

This will help you win points in both situations.

DEFENSIVE POINTS

- Rally speed →	% tennis
- Pattern of play →	Consistency
	Smart patterns

OFFENSIVE POINTS

- Easy ball shots →	
- Open court shots →	Be brave and go for it!
- Approach shots →	

THIRTEEN: BE MENTALLY TOUGH AND LEARN FROM YOUR MISTAKES.

Follow an error analysis:

1. Did your opponent hit too good a shot?
2. Did you rush your shot?
3. Did you try to hit too hard?
4. Did you chose the wrong technique?
    a. On a low short ball
    b. On a ball halfway between a volley and an overhead

The occasional outburst following an error is okay. Let your opponent know you've come to play. As long as the verbal outburst is motivational, instructional, and positive.

Example of no: I am so bad, I always miss that shot. I suck eggs through a straw.

Example of yes: Take your time, don't rush the stroke when you get an easy ball.

You can throw your racquet when you're a little frustrated—up in the air and catch it but not down to the court and smash it.

FOURTEEN: IMPROVEMENT IN TENNIS IS IN DIRECT RELATION-SHIP TO:

a) The number of balls hit

b) Practicing smart, well thought-out drills

c) Playing practice matches

d) Playing tournament matches

e) Recognizing that a complete player is full bottle in the four areas of:

    a. Strokes

    b. Strategies

    c. Physical fitness

    d. Mental toughness

When taking a look at the player's match rallying situations, find out what interactions the players engage in most, especially considering the style of play of today's game.

Most time spent (in decreasing order) for a singles match:

1. Baseline to baseline rallying

2. The battle between the server and the receiver

3. Hitting approach shots

4. Hitting passing shots

5. Volley to volley

Once a player has matured to have acceptable strokes and strategies, perhaps this realization of rallying times would help determine the practice schedule emphasis.

Two useful statistics to study:

1. What strokes or strategies your next opponent uses to win most of their points.
2. What strokes or strategies you use to play your most successful matches.

Chapter 3

Singles Tips: Things That Matter and Will Make a Difference

WHEN PREPARING FOR YOUR MATCHES

a) Mentally and physically, start preparing the night before—racquets, towels, water container, hat, sunblock, and smart snacks. Where are you playing? What time is the match? Who is driving you to the match?

b) Get pumped up and excited to play. Re-watch a great tennis match on TV. Listen to some upbeat music. Do whatever it takes to get you pumped up and excited to play.

    a. 10/10 pumped up is too high. If overly excited to play, players tend to rush their shots and/or try to hit the ball too hard.

    b. 2/10 pumped up is too low. 1/10 is sleeping, so 2/10 is just a shade above sleeping.

    c. Be an 8/10, which is a nice blend of excited to play and being under control.

c) Get to the match site early so you can "acclimatize" to the conditions. For example:

    a. The type and playability of the courts.

    b. The number and proximity of possible spectators.

    c. The weather conditions. Windy? Hot?

    d. There could be some noise from a nearby playground or roadway.

d) Check in with the tournament desk early and avoid a hectic last-minute rush.

e) When arriving and walking onto your match court, stamp your foot on the court and say under your breath, "This is my court, and this is my day."

MAYBE I'M TOO EARLY!

26 SINGLES TIPS

1. Determine what type of player is coming at you. Watch your opponent warming up—playing style and possible weaknesses.

2. Your first job is to get organized and as comfortable as possible—footwork and racquet preparation.

3. Analyze the oncoming ball and ask the question: to hit or not to hit? In other words, hit a grooved shot or improvise.

4. Hit with your rally speed—as high as you can without missing—a little short of a winner.

OOPS! TOO SOFT!   AH....H! JUST RIGHT!   NUTS ! TOO HARD!

5. Start with your favorite patterns of play and add some patterns that will hurt your opponent.

6. Have a desperateness to keep the ball going. Don't go for quick winners. Wait for a mistake by your opponent or an easy ball you can hurt your opponent with.

7. It is more important to hit groundstrokes and first volleys *deep* rather than to go with power.

8. Just as quickly as you move off to hit a shot, recover to home base or to a smart strategic spot. You must assume your opponent will get the ball back. Pretend you have been pulled back to "home base" by a giant magnet.

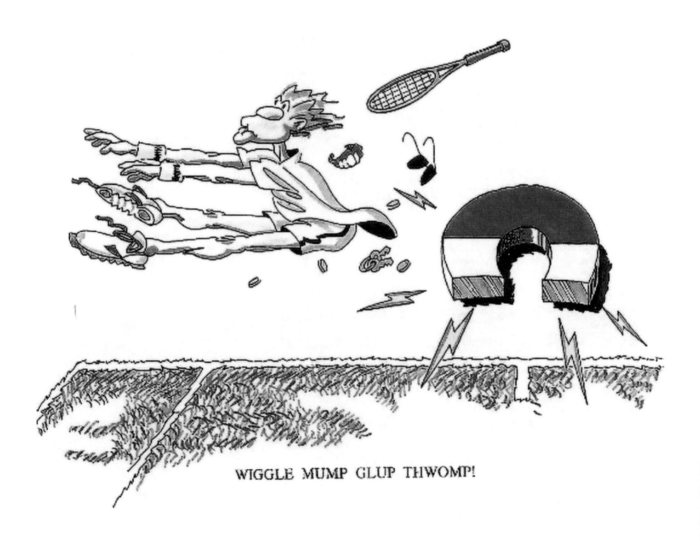

WIGGLE MUMP GLUP THWOMP!

9. Recognize the color of the ball coming at you: yellow = rally; red = improvise, green = go for it. What color are you most likely to get? Recognize the yellow, take care of the red, and look forward to the green.

10. Look for opportunities to "cut" your opponent's sidelines—that will give you three chances to win the point.

    a. They cannot get to the ball.

    b. They make a mistake.

    c. They struggle to get the ball back, but the whole court is open for you to hit into.

    d. Cross court drives are easier and safer for you to hit, and you have a shorter recovery to the middle of the angle.

11. When you get an easy ball, remember you don't have to break the ball. Make a wise choice:

    a. Go for a winning drive into a corner (a combination of speed and angle)

    b. Hit into the open court. If cross court, go with the angle. If down the line, go with speed and depth.

    c. Hit an approach shot or a drop shot.

12. If the court is really wide open, remember, "You don't need an elephant gun to kill a squirrel." You can hit a "safer" shot.

DRAT ! I OVERDID IT !

13. If playing a hustler – you may have to hit "two winning shots" rather than going for one risky "too aggressive" shot.

14. It is smart to lob back when you are chasing down a lob. You can assume your opponent will come to the net.

15. It is smart to drop shot a drop shot if your opponent is on the baseline.

16. When hitting an inside-out forehand, angle is important. When hitting an inside-in forehand, speed and depth are more important (you have been pulled wide and have left the whole court open). A much more aggressive shot is needed.

17. When forced to hit a difficult shot because you are out of position, off balance, or uncomfortable, place your shot to a spot your opponent cannot hurt you— deep down the middle or sliced low and off to the sides.

18. If driven wide on your forehand side, defensively hit a high topspin drive cross court (or a winning shot down the line). If driven wide on your backhand, defensively hit a slice cross court, either short or deep. If pulled extremely wide off court, go for a winner or a giant, deep lob.

19. Donut Theory. Pretend your opponent's court is in the shape of a donut. Aim for the donut—deep, wide, or short—not in the donut hole (which is the middle of the court). Avoid giving your opponent a "cupcake."

20. Approach shots

    a. Hit them at the right time. When you are moving into the court, on balance, and looking at a comfortable mid-court ball (not quite the right ball to hit a winner on).

    b. To be effective, come in on the right ball and hurt your opponent with the shot.

    c. Pick a target (weak side, open court, down the middle at your opponent).

    d. Stroke selection (heavy topspin, deep landing, power drive, side spin slice drive.

e. Follow the ball flight to the net and remember to split step.

f. On the approach shot, think deep, on the volley angle off.

g. If your net shot is difficult, hit deep down the line or drop shot.

h. If the net shot is a "cupcake," close in and angle off the volley. You don't need a lot of speed if an angle shot is going to win the point. You close in to hit but not too close to stand.

l. When approaching on a short, wide ball, approach down the line (or hit a sharp angle cross court).

21. Passing shots

a. You are target-shooting down the line. Your target is a rectangle, the full length of the court, speed ball "rip" (opponent will angle off a slow drive)

- Cross court – a triangle "dip"
- Forehand – hit with topspin
- Backhand – hit with topspin or slice
- Close in as soon as you see your opponent's contact is below the net.

b. Recovery after your passing shot:

- The better your pass – edge toward the net
- An average pass – recover to home base
- A horrible pop-up pass – run hard to the open court net post, not along the baseline.
- Hit and move somewhere – no standing to admire your shot!

c. After hitting a couple of passing shots, an offensive lob becomes a good choice, as your opponent will usually close in. Keep your head down when lobbing to avoid showng your intent.

d. If chasing a short ball to try and pass, an angle shot or lob is wise—or straight at your opponent—not with the idea of hurting them but to force an error.

e. When facing a serve-and-volley player, you may want to mix in dropping your return at their feet, then pass their pop-up shot.

f. Pass or lob, no cupcakes (the easy ball between a drive and a lob).

22. Work on developing both defensive and offensive skills so you can win points in both situations.

23. If you are losing 90% of the baseline rallies:

a. Start mixing up your shots

- Mostly drive with your rally speed.
- Occasionally hit a high deep heavy topspin drive.
- Occasionally hit a short slider. This will interrupt your opponent's rhythm and keep them guessing.

b. Slow down the pace of the match.

- Take the full 20 seconds between points
- Take the full 1.5 minutes at changeovers

There are many ways to lose a match, so you might as well try them all.

24. Yes, do show emotion but make it positive, instructional, or motivational. The occasional verbal outburst is *okay*. Let your opponent know you have come to play.

25. Yes! You can throw your racquet *up* in the air to catch it but not *down* to the court to smash it.

26. Improvement in tennis is in direct relationship to:

a. The number of balls hit

b. Practicing smart and well-thought-out drills

c. Playing practice matches

d. Playing tournament matches

Shot Selection and Stroke Adjustments (you are receiving the ball)
Baseline to Baseline

A) Rally Speed
1) Windshield wiper, backfoot
2) Deep followed by short aim
    to the weak side

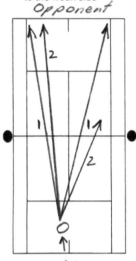

B) High Bounce
1. On the rise
2. Back up / or swing volley /
    overhead

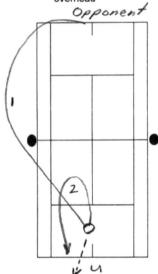

C) Short Ball
1. Slow topspin roll
2. Slice deep or short
3. Drop shot, angle

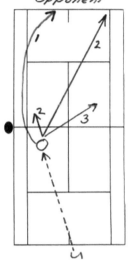

D) Wide to Forehand
Heavy topspin, high, cross court

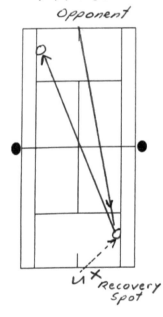

E) Wide to Backhand
Slice cross court

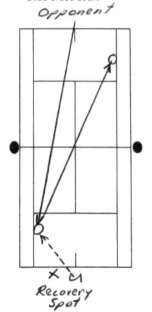

F) Fast Approaching
1) Short backswing drive
2) Slice back deep

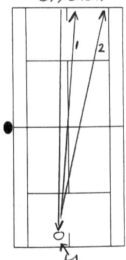

Opponent at Baseline, You are at the Net (you are hitting the ball)

A) Tough Shot (low, wide)
1) Deep down the line
2) Short angle shot or
3) Deep to weak side

B) Easy Ball Approaching
1. Close in to angle off
2. Drop shot short

C) Opponent Lobs You
1. Short lob – close in overhead
2. Deep lob – back up

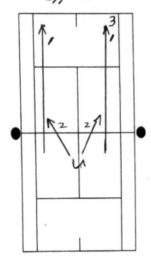
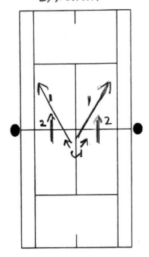
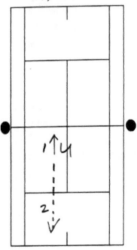

Opponent at the Net, You Are at the Baseline (you are hitting the ball)

A) You Hit A Great Lob
Close to the net (not too close, most often a lob will come back)

B) You are Pulled Wide
1) Speed down the line
2) Angle cross court
3) Lob
4) No cupcakes

C) Regular Passing Shot
1) Speed down the line
2) Angle cross court
3) Lob
4) No cupcakes

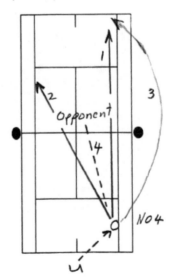
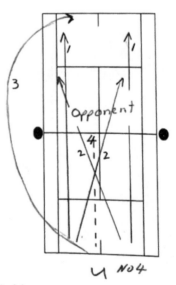

Definition of a Cupcake: An easy ball popped up to a net player halfway between a drive and a lob.

CONTROLLING NERVES

Who gets nervous before a match?

1. Players get nervous before a match because they care about what's happening.

2. Everyone gets nervous. Tell yourself you are going to be a little less nervous than your opponent.

3. Stan Smith was quoted as saying, "I get nervous when I'm not nervous—that means I don't care."

4. Nerves usually go away with time.

5. Some match tips to try out to help settle your nerves:

    a. Get to the match early so you can adjust to the conditions.

    b. Get into the point comfortably with your first serve in and returned back.

    c. Hit "vanilla" shots safely down the middle.

    d. Most nervous players are robotic and don't move efficiently. They should be encouraged to move a lot in the warm-up period and talk to someone so they come out of their shell.

    e. Take the 20 seconds between points and the 90 seconds at changeovers to reflect and review your simple game plan. Plan to get four balls over in a row.

    f. Sit relaxed at changeovers and breathe deeply.

    g. To stay focused, it helps to say, under your breath, "hit" as you hit the ball and "bounce" and then "hit" as your opponent hits the ball.

    h. Between points, sing your favorite song (under your breath, of course!).

    i. Let your opponent serve first, giving you time to relax before you have to serve.

BUILDING CONFIDENCE

Who has a better chance to win a match? A player that is *not* very confident or a player that *is* confident?

Confidence is a belief in yourself, always positive, never doubting your ability. Confidence is a belief that you can play tennis very well.

Research has indicated that the most consistent factor distinguishing highly successful players from less successful is confidence.

BUILDING CONFIDENCE – THE BIG TWO

1. Preparation. In four areas: strokes, strategies, physical fitness, and mental toughness. Preparation is true for most things, e.g., studying for a math exam, preparing for a dinner party, and preparing for a tennis tournament. Improvement in tennis is directly related to the number of balls hit.

2. Self-talk. If doing well in a drill, a practice match, or a tournament match, take the time to give yourself a pat on the back (drop your racquet over your shoulder and pat yourself). Too often, players get down on themselves if things are not going well. So be fair to yourself and be positive, self-instructional, self-motivational, and self-talk when you're doing well.

PATTERNS OF PLAY

Serve Placement Patterns

I placed a ladder behind the notch at the baseline and climbed up the ladder to see what part of the service boxes I could see over the net first. It was targets 4 and 5 (these targets then would be the flat power serves). I'm guessing that a player taller than 6'6" could hit a flat power serve to all the targets, with the possible exception of targets 1 and 8.

8 Serve Placement Targets

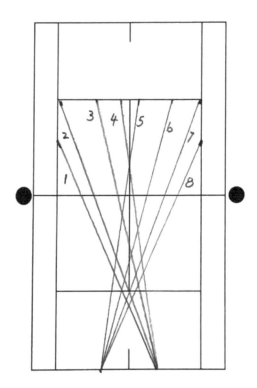

1. Topspin / slice pull off court

2. Can flatten it out

3. Fast slice into body

4. Power, flat speed serve (or heavy slice into the body)

5. Power, flat speed serve

6. Slice into body

7. Can flatten it out

8. Heavy topspin – pull off court

Patterns of Play – You Are Hitting the Ball

① Windshield wiper and backfooting

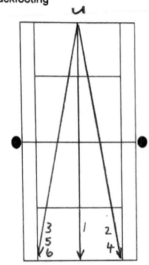

1-Deep
2,3,4,5,6-Cross court then backfoot

② High, deep drive, followed by a short shot

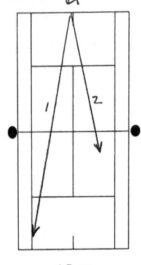

1-Deep
2-Short

③ Focusing on a target then a quick change of direction

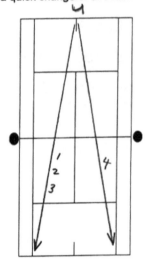

1,2,3 to backhand
4 to open court

④

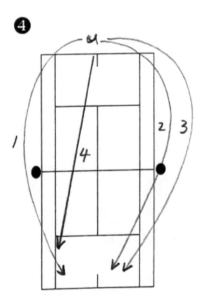

1,2,3-High and deep
4-short slider
Focusing on a target then a quick change of direction

⑤

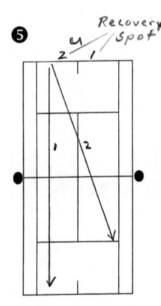

1-Forehand down the line
2-Forehand short drive cross court
Deep drive followed by an angle shot

⑥

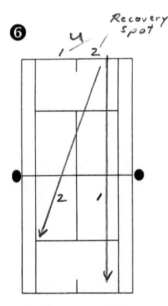

1-Backhand down the line
2-backhand short drive cross court
Deep drive followed by an angle shot

Patterns of Play – You Are Hitting the Ball

7 Deep shot down the middle followed by an angle drive

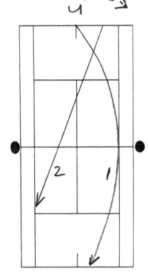

1-Deep middle
2-Inside out forehand

8 Deep ball to backhand followed by inside out to backhand (or inside in)

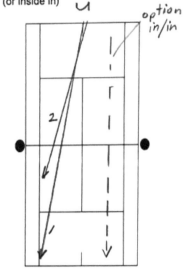

option in/in

1-Backhand cross court
2-Backhand short drive cross court

9 You mix up deep/wide/short (fast-slice)

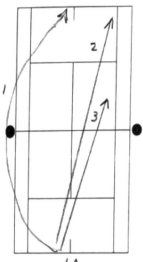

U mix shots
1. DEEP
2. FAST
3. SHORT

❿

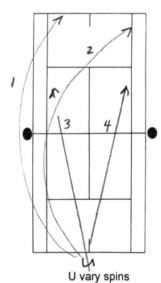

U vary spins
1,2 Topspin
3,4 Slice
(be unpredictable)

⓫ Weaker bakchand

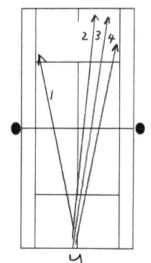

More shots to weaker side 2, 3, 4
All shot to weak side then surprise an open court shot to 1

⓬

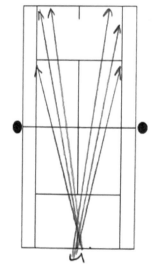

Hit all shots cross court (either open court or backfoot) that will really move your opponent

Patterns of Play – You Are Hitting the Ball

❶❸ Serve wide to get an open court shot

← Opponent

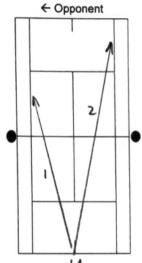

U serve
Serve a "1" serve
2 approach shot
If easy, in/out or in/in
If good return, rally

❶❹ Serve wide to get an open court shot

Opponent →

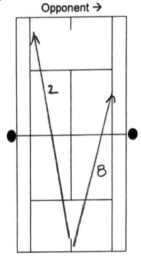

U serve
Serve an "8" serve
2 approach shot
If easy in/out or in/in
If good return, rally

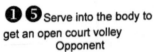

❶❺ Serve into the body to get an open court volley

Opponent

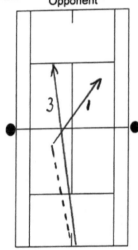

You S&V
A "3" serve
1 open court volley
If tough, return hit deep down the line or short

❶❻

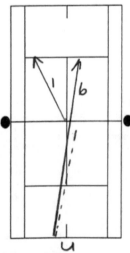

You serve and volley
A "6" serve
1 open court volley
If tough, return hit deep down the line or short
Serve into the body to get an open court volley

❶❼

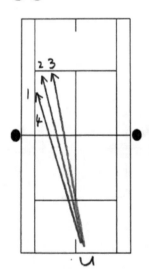

U serve & V
1, 2 or 3 serve
4 Volley short to backfoot
Serve wide then backfoot the volley

❶❽

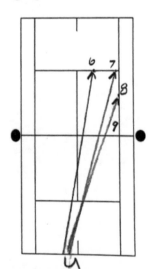

U serve & V
6, 7, 8 serve
9 Volley short to backfoot
Serve wide then backfoot the volley

Patterns of Play – You Are Hitting the Ball

① ⑨ Easy serve
Opponent Serving

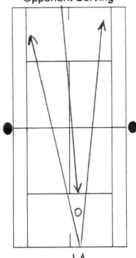

Returning serve
Hit aggressively to corners

② ⓪ Tough serve
Opponent Serving

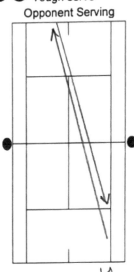

Returning serve
Deep down the middle

② ① Easy serve
Opponent Serving and
Volleying

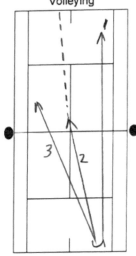

Returning serve
1 – rip
2 – at feet
3 – angle (dip)

② ② Tough serve
Opponent Serving and
Volleying

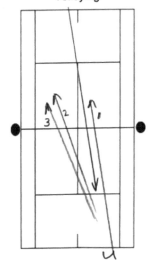

Returning serve
1 – low at the feet
2, 3 – cross court
Set up for a passing shot

POSSIBLE PATTERNS OF PLAY

You choose

1, 2, 3, 4, 5, 6, 7, 8, 9, 10, 11, 12

Losing most baseline rallies

Mix up shots

9, 10, 11, 12

You serve

Stay at the baseline

13, 14

You serve and volley

15, 16, 17, 19

Opponent serving and staying at the baseline

19, 20

Opponent serving and volleying

21, 22

PLAYING A PUSHER

a. Getting an open court shot

1, 2, 3, 4, 7, 8, 9, 11, 12, 13, 14

b. Pulling them to the net

2, 4, 8, 9, 19 (19 could be a drop shot)

c. You are approaching the net

15, 16, 17, 18

Playing a Slugger

a. Keep them rallying

b. Mix up shots

Playing a Slow Mover

a. Run them north and south (deep and then short)

b. Run them east and west side to side and occasionally backfoot)

Playing a Player with a Dominating Forehand

a. Hit wide to forehand to open up the next shot to attack their backhand

b. Mix up shots (high, wide, short) to force an opponent to hit more uncomfortable shots

Some Thoughts

You will feel more comfortable hitting your preferred patterns of play. Add in some patterns of play that would hurt your opponent. Take advantage of any shortcomings or weaknesses they may have.

PLAYING ON CLAY (POINTS TO CONSIDER)

Don't freak out. Tennis is tennis, whether you play on a hard court, clay court, a parking lot, or the deck of a ship. You hit serves, forehands, backhands, overheads, and drop shots, no matter what surface you play on.

So, keep your game plan of "controlled aggressiveness" and keep in mind the following:

1. The surface is labeled "slow." It's tougher to put the ball away, so be patient to set up your point. You can get to more tough shots than you think you can. Don't give up on wide balls. Change your grips and hit the ball back deep down the middle (deep down the middle is okay—it's short down the middle for which you will have to say, "Nice shot.")

2. Unpredictable bounces often occur, so pay attention to setting up well.

3. Mentally prepare to develop the point. Be patient and wait for the opening.

4. If you get a chance to hit a winner, go for it! (either open court or short ball).

5. Slide / Hit or Run Run Run Run Slide / Hit. When sliding, make a solid plant on the weight-bearing foot.

◊   Wide backhands – slide onto the right foot.

◊   Wide forehands – stay open and slide onto the right foot.

6. Because of the difficulty in changing direction, wrong foot a lot (hit behind your opponent).

7. Difficult to speed ball through the baseline. Use sidelines more – use short corner balls a lot.

8. Hit deep drives over the net, usually topspin. Depth is more important on clay.

9. Take spins well—mostly drive, but mix it up, occasionally hit high topspin drives or short "sidespin slice" sliders.

10. Only come to the net if the opportunity is a good one. Hit angle volleys, short volleys, or deep volleys. The in-between volleys will get ripped.

11. Side spin / slice approach shots are effective since the ball will stay low.

12. Use drop shots at the right time – off the same ball you would hit an approach shot on – or when returning a soft serve.

13. When you receive a drop shot or a short ball, run hard to get up alongside the ball:

    a) Sidespin slice down the line

    b) Topspin roll deep

    c) Sharp angle cross court

Or, if the shot is comfortable, or the ball comes up above net height, hit a winner.

14. If being destroyed by a pusher, eliminate the long baseline to baseline rallies. You come in at an opportune time and pull them in by hitting them a cheap drop shot.

15. If being air-balled to death:

    a) Hit on the upbounce (on the rise)

    b) Slice

    c) Move up to volley

    d) Drop short balls on them so they cannot bloop.

16. Place your serve well – pull them off the court, slice to deuce side, kick to ad. Serve into the body.

17. Play like a clay master!

Two Player Singles Drills (no coach is involved in the drills)
Groundstrokes → (consistency and placement)

❶

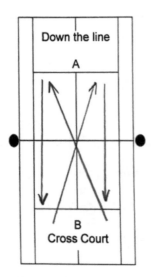

Change after a few minutes
(rallying in the service box)

❷

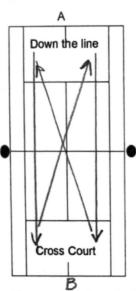

Change after a few minutes
(rallying full court)

Point Play →

❸ A hits all shots to the
Ad side →

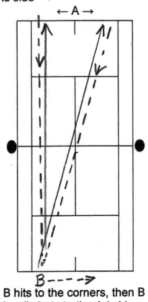

B hits to the corners, then B
hits all shots to the Ad side
and A hits to the corners

❹ B hits all shot to the Deuce
side →→→

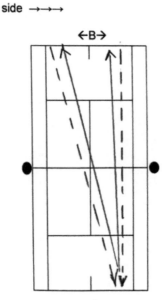

A hits to corners then A hits
all shots to Deuce side and B
hits to the corners

❺

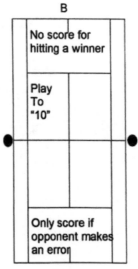

Comfortable feed to start the
point

❻

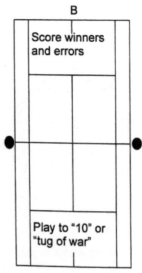

Comfortable feed to start the
point

7 Match play – only one serve.

8 Take it in turns to start down 30-0.

9 If one player is more advanced, have the developing player take one point (at any time they choose—except on game point).

❶⓿ Down the Line Approach Shots (practice both down the line approaches)

B

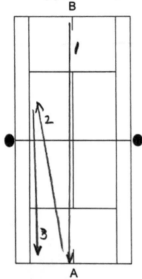

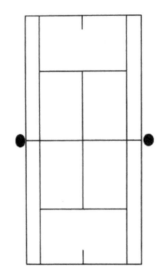

A

1 – B feeds to A
2 - A drops the ball short
3 - B hits and approach shot down the line.
Play the point out (switch ends)

❶❶ Passing Shots

B

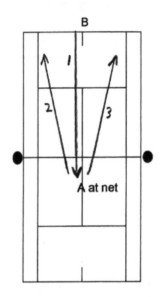

1 – B feeds to A
2 – A volleys to Deuce side, plays point out
3 – Next feed A volleys to Ad side (switch ends)

❶❷ Volley to Volley – chase ball down

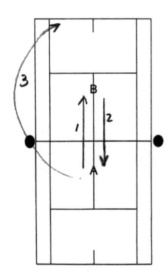

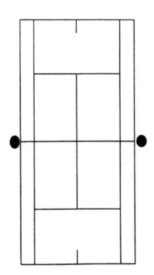

1 – A cooperative volley
2 - B cooperative volley
3 – A lobs over B, play the point out (players take turns to lob)

❶❸ Overhead Practice

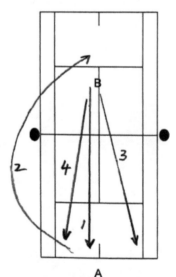

A

1 – B feed to A
2 – A lobs to B
3 – B overheads to Deuce side
4 – Next lob from A, B overheads to Ad side (play the point out)

Chapter 4

Observations on Match Play

(Notes jotted down while observing my students play matches to discuss as teaching points later.)

WARM UP – STARTING AND FINISHING POINTS

1. Rally friendly baseline to baseline, move around as much as you can, and, where possible, talk to feel relaxed and like you belong!

2. Realistic warmup to accentuate footwork, hit slices and topspins. If your opponent leaves momentarily to towel off or get something, simulate hitting groundstrokes/serves.

3. Take turns coming to the net to volley (still hitting friendly). Ask for some lobs so you can warm up your overheads.

4. Both warmup serve at the same time.

a. Serve to both sides/hit some first serves and second serves.

b. Block back some of the opponent's serves to warm up.

5. The server calls out the score loudly before serving so any disagreements can be cleared up.

6. Make line calls both verbally and visually.

7. On a close line call, you may hit the ball back to your opponent and immediately call "out" (if, in fact, the ball was out!).

8. When your opponent hits a passing shot, and you don't get a good look at the ball bounce, you may ask your opponent for help with the call.

9. If the opponent's serve is well out, don't return the serve. Block the ball softly into the net, or let their serve pass you by.

10. Simple game plan—keep the ball going, wait for a mistake from your opponent or an opportunity for you to finish the point.

11. Look for possible stroke weaknesses and note your opponent's playing style (so you can plan your strategies).

SERVING

1. Get a high percentage of first services *in* (Your opponent is more likely to make a mistake or return your first serve with a less aggressive shot. If missing too many first serves, serve very fast second serves as first serves.

2. After serving, be ready to move, watch what the serve has done and be ready to anticipate (no standing passively watching the return!)

3. Mix up serves (have some favorite go-to's):

    a. Pull your opponent off the court with a slice to the deuce side or a kick serve to the ad side.

    b. Aim your serve to your opponent's backhand or weaker side.

    c. Serve into your opponent's body.

4. Too many double faults – serve fast second serves.

5. Power serves should be hit down the T.

6. No rush when serving – have a smooth, controlled routine. Organize your stance, bounce the ball a few times. Point your racquet at the service box and talk to your opponent under your breath: "This ball is not coming back."

7. Take time to compose before serving your second serve.

RECEIVING SERVE

1. When receiving an extremely fast first serve, just be happy to block the ball back deep down the middle of the court and get into the point.

2. Hit more aggressively when returning second serves:

   a. Return to opponent's weak side.

   b. Return into the corners.

   c. Hit an approach shot and approach the net.

3. If your opponent is serving and volleying, you have two choices:

   a. Go for an immediate passing shot, a speed ball down the line, or a sharply angled cross court return.

   b. Hit a low, short return at your opponent's feet, hopefully getting a pop-up to get an easier ball to pass them.

4. Server has the advantage—get the return in play.

5. Visibly close in when setting up to return the second serve.

6. Occasionally, go for a second serve return winner if you are playing well or you get a comfortable, easy ball.

BASELINE RALLIES

1. The first thing to do is get your rally speed going. Hit the ball as hard as you can without missing, a little short of a winner.

2. Use the patterns of play you feel comfortable with. For example, corner to corner, then backfoot. Add some patterns that would hurt your opponent's weaknesses.

3. Anticipate when you have hurt your opponent and expect an opportunity to be aggressive—to approach the net or hit a winner.

4. If receiving a difficult approaching ball (high topspin, very wide, very fast), hit a safe, solid hang-in-there shot, i.e., deep down the middle or sliced angle.

KRRRRRR...MAYBE IT WASN'T A SMASH!

5. If pulled too wide and not coming back into the court, go for a winner drive or lob if your opponent is at the net.

6. If missing easy balls, ask the questions: Too much speed? Rushing shots? Wrong shot? Not getting set up comfortably? Shot selection?

7. More care and safety when hitting on the rise shots.

8. Many ways to get a mistake from your opponent or get an easy ball.

    a. High-bouncing, deep, topspin drive

    b. Low-bouncing, angled slider

    c. Windshield wiper, then occasionally backfoot

    d. Cut sidelines to pull your opponent off the court (with a serve, groundstroke, or volley)

    e. Keep your shots out of your opponent's comfortable hitting zones

9. Be brave when you get an easy ball.

    a. Go for a winning shot to the corners (a blend of speed and placement)

    b. Hit an approach shot

    c. Cut the sideline

    d. Hit a drop shot

10. Commit to getting to every ball. Force your opponent to hit 2-3 winning shots to win the point.

11. Spend enough time on each shot and recover quickly (to home base or a tactically smart spot). You can watch to see how your shot was as you are recovering. You must assume the ball is coming back.

12. The three traffic lights concept: the ball approaches at three different speeds. Match up the three speeds with the three traffic lights.

   a. Yellow traffic light (caution) – most common = rally speed

   b. Red traffic light (stop or danger) – tough shot, fast, wide, high = improvise

   c. Green traffic light (go) – easy ball, be aggressive = go for it

13. Pick a target for your green light put away shot. It will give the stroke more purpose. Rush to get to the ball, then compose yourself to put the ball away.

14. Don't hit *big* shots if the ball is way deep behind the baseline (high drive back).

15. With your opponent off the court, your open court winning shot doesn't have to be hit with a lot of speed. Angle off your shot. You don't need an elephant gun to kill a squirrel. Speed and angle don't mix very well. That combination can look very ugly, kind of like watching lemon juice being poured into milk.

16. What strategies to use when playing an opponent with exemplary groundstrokes. You are being destroyed by ball speed and placement. Hit your shots to difficult places for them to get comfortable so they cannot use their strong groundstrokes against you. Try some of these ideas to see what might work best.

   a. Hit high, deep-landing, high-bouncing drives and mix in some short sliders occasionally (if you force them really deep).

   b. Hit *all* your drives cross court for periods of time. That will stretch your opponent out, forcing them to hit more uncomfortable groundstrokes.

   c. Throw in a continuous mixture of spins at your opponent—heavy topspins, slices, side spins. They will have a more difficult time grooving the strokes that are hurting you.

d. Say you are receiving a short, easy ball. Approach the net or pull them to the net to take them out of their aggressive baseline hitting. This forces them to hit passing shots under pressure or to have to receive your bullet passing shots.

e. Fake an injury and limp off the court.

APPROACHING THE NET

1. When moving in for an easy ball shot, decide whether you want to hit a winner or hit an approach shot.

   a. Winner = speed and angle/drop shot

   b. Approach = will finish with a volley or an overhead. Think of an approach shot as being a little short of a winner.

2. Mix up your approach shots:

   a. Speed to corners

   b. High, deep, heavy topspin

   c. Side spin slice

   d. To weak side

   e. To open court

3. On a short, wide ball, hit the approach shot:

   a. Down the line *or*

   b. Sharp angle cross court

   c. Lob if your opponent is tight at net

4. Approaching down the middle will take away a possible sharp angle passing shot.

5. If easy ball is low or you are off balance, hit an approach shot.

6. Run fast to at least get into the service box – split step, pause, then move to volley.

7. From a standing-at-net position, make a quick, short jump and rebound to move to a volley.

    a. One-step volley (if the incoming ball is close)

    b. Skip-step volley (If the incoming ball is a little further away)

    c. When receiving an extremely wide passing shot, dive onto a one-leg volley (onto the right leg when going to either the forehand or backhand side)

8. Spend enough time on and stay down when hitting half volleys or low volleys. Half volley only when you have to. You are usually better off choosing to back up and drive or close in to volley.

9. When you get a tough, difficult shot of any kind at the net, your best option is to hit deep down the line or hit a drop shot.

10. When receiving an easy volley, close in and angle off. Aim for the open court service box so your volley cuts across the sideline fairly close to the net.

11. Every now and then, surprise your opponent by serving and volleying on your first serve.

HITTING PASSING SHOTS

1. You don't have to break the ball or land the ball on the line. Think of passing shots as more of a placement shot.

2. Passing down the line is more of a speed shot. The target area is a long rectangle the whole length of the court with the ball crossing the baseline. Cross court passing shots are more of a placement shot, the target is a triangle shape, with the passing shots cutting the sideline. The stroke emphasis can be described as:

    a. Down the line – you rip

    b. Cross court – you dip

3. After a couple of passing shots, a lob is a good choice.

4. Straight at the net player (either a speed ball or a low ball at the feet) is an option to get an error.

5. Hit and move somewhere!

    a. Better pass – edge in

    b. Average pass – recover to the middle

    c. Horrible pass – run into the open court towards the net post. If you run along the baseline, it's a longer distance to the ball contact point.

6. Choose to hit a passing shot. If not comfortable or off balance, then lob. No shots in between a drive or a lob. In other words, don't give your opponent an easy ball to put away. Don't give your opponent a cupcake; they will eat it up.

MISCELLANEOUS THOUGHTS

1. If emotionally unraveling due to these possibilities:

    i. Balking a little when about to serve for the set or match

    ii. You are making too many unforced errors

    iii. Opponent is hitting too many winners

Try these two possible solutions:

    i. Take 20 seconds to settle down and figure out how to feel or do better. Am I rushing shots? Hitting too big?

    ii. Should I try to first keep four balls in the court before looking to hit a winning shot?

2. Match pace – no rush between points – a confident stride. No rush to serve (have a routine).

  a. Winning – keep the match pace upbeat

  b. Losing – slow the match pace and think of possible adjustments

3. Positive release of frustration is okay. Hit racquet up and catch it. Slap leg with your hand.

4. 90% of points are over in the first five hits.

  a. Serve / Serve return / Server's shot / Receiver's shot / Server's shot

  b. Hit a lot of first serves in and a lot of returns back

5. If nervous, hit vanilla shots (safe and deep down the middle). Overly move. Avoid moving like a robot. Talk when you can to relax emotionally.

6. Etiquette – if a serve is out by a lot, don't return to opponent.

7. Make a quick analysis of the opponent's winners and your mistakes. Figure out some adjustments you could make.

8. Move at a controlled match pace. No rush to finish the match quickly.

IMPORTANT CONCEPTS

Consistency – keep the ball going.

Really Hustle – have a desperateness to get each ball back over the net. Force your opponent to hit two to three winning shots to win the point.

Defensive Skills – slice, block lob when you have to.

Develop Offensive Tactics – force your opponent into making mistakes or giving you opportunities to win the point.

Physical Fitness – so you move the same way at the close of a long match as you did in the first few games.

Mental Toughness – calm but aggressive mind.

The Name of Your Game Plan – Controlled Aggressiveness

WHAT DO YOU DO WHEN...? (A QUESTION AND ANSWER GUIDE)

As a player and coach, I have encountered and observed several challenging situations to navigate during the course of a match. This guidance is based on USTA/ITF regulations and my experience.

1. <u>How do you start a match?</u>

You flip a coin or spin a racquet to see who chooses one of four options.

    a. Serve

    b. Receive serve

    c. Choose a side

    d. Defer

2. <u>How do you make line calls?</u>

Call your side of the court. Call verbally "out" and do a visual hand signal (index finger in the air) if out. Flat hand out to the side if the ball was in.

    a. If you cannot make the call immediately, it was in.

    b. If you are at the net and get passed and don't get a good look at the ball bounce, you can ask your opponent for help with the call. Hardly watch where the ball lands if clearly "in" or "out." If the bounce is going to be close, open your eyes wide and really watch the ball bounce.

    c. If you think you are getting bad calls, ask your opponent, "Are you sure it was out?" (Do not ask all the time). If bad calls persist, at a break in play, visit the Tournament Director and be tactful. Don't say, "That little 'schnick' is giving me bad calls." Say, "We are having trouble with line calls," and ask for a "line judge." Players have to ask the line judge for a ruling.

3. <u>Who calls a "let" serve?</u>

Either player.

4. <u>Who calls "double bounce?"</u>

The player that has the ball coming at them.

5. <u>What happens if the wrong player serves the first few points in a game?</u>

The score stands – make the correction.

6. <u> If you see your opponent foot faulting, can you make the call?</u>

No, you can warn them and, if it persists, call for an umpire to watch your match.

7. <u>What do you do when, after a few points have been played, you realize a doubles team has been receiving from the wrong side?</u>

The score stands – make the correction.

8. <u>What happens when you touch the net while the ball is in play?</u>

You lose the point.

9. <u>What happens when the ball is in play, and your hat falls off your head and hits the net?</u>

You lose the point.

10. <u>Can you "carry" the ball if you "double hit?"</u>

Yes, if your stroke is one swing.

11. <u>What happens when the ball hits you while still in play, even if you are standing outside the court?</u>

You lose the point.

12. <u>What happens when the ball in play hits a ball on the court?</u>

You lose the point unless you return the ball after it has bounced once.

13. <u>Can you ever reach over the net to hit the ball?</u>

   a. Yes, only if the ball has landed in your court first and is returning to your opponent's court.

   b. Once the ball is contacted on your side, your follow through may be onto your opponent's side, but the racquet can never touch the net during play.

14. <u>Can you hit a shot around the net post?</u>

Yes. Also, if your shot hits the net post and lands in your opponent's court, play on.

15. <u>What happens when a ball rolls onto your court during a rally, and it distracts you?</u>

Stop play, raise your hand, and call, "Let, please."

16. <u>What happens if your opponent is quick-serving you before you are ready?</u>

Immediately raise your hand and call, "Let, please." Make no attempt to hit the ball back.

17. <u>What do you do if your opponent is overly jumping around to distract your serve?</u>

At a break in play, call for an umpire to monitor your match.

18. <u>What do you do when you and your opponent have both lost track of the score?</u>

Go back to where you can agree on the score. Otherwise, start the game over.

Chapter 5

Playing Smart Doubles

DOUBLES STRATEGIES THAT WILL MAKE A DIFFERENCE

INTRODUCTION

If an alien from another planet were to come to Earth and watch a doubles match for the first time, it would look like two players having a fun rally and another two players trying to ruin their fun!

If you come off the court having lost a singles match, there is no question you are a loser. In doubles, there are some things you can do to help yourself look good:

1. Get a good partner.
2. If in trouble during a rally, yell, "Yours!" real loud, and you are off the hook. Your partner has to get the ball.
3. After a losing doubles match (and making sure your partner cannot hear you), you can announce, "If only my partner had gotten just a couple of serve returns back in play."
4. Get the side of the court you like to return from. With a new partner, hustle out to take up a ready position on the side you prefer to return from. Your partner will be too embarrassed to say, "I want to play on the side you wanted," and you will get to play on your preferred side.

5. The cardinal sin in doubles is to pop up an easy ball to the opposing net players. Players must be able to hit strokes across the court and away from the opposing net player. A quick mechanics check on hitting drives across the court:

CONSIDER A RIGHT-HANDER

a. Hitting from the deuce side:

i. **Forehand**: Open stance (face the net a little more), short backswing, ball contact early.

ii. **Backhand**: Closed stance (turn sideways a lot), ball contact a little later.

b. Hitting from the ad side:

i. **Forehand**: Closed stance (turn sideways a lot), ball contact a little later.

ii. **Backhand**: Open stance (face the net a little more), short backswing, ball contact early.

TIPS

1. Choosing a partner:

a. Like each other as people.

b. Respect each other as players.

c. You both receive serve from the side you prefer to return serve.

2. Watch your opponents closely in the warmup. Note the weaker player.

3. Freeze out the opponents' best player.

4. Your most experienced (better) player should play the ad side. There are more game points played on that side (6 vs. 2). The ad side player has to hit more backhands and cover three-fourths of the court hitting overheads.

5. The player most likely to hold serve should serve first. In a 6-4 set, the starting server has served one more time.

6. Much talk (e.g., mine, yours, leave it) during rallies.

7. Positive communication between points (e.g., "Good job!") if your partner plays a great point. High-five each other when celebrating or encouraging each other.

8. Communicate with "we" coaching. For example, "We should get to the net more," or "We should mix in some lobs with our passing shots." No individual coaching (unless asked by your partner). It is not a good idea to say to your partner, "You are not turning your hips enough on your groundstrokes."

9. Help each other with line calls, on serve returns, and when receiving deep balls approaching the baseline. Remember you can hit a shot and then immediately call out.

10. If told to play more aggressively, what does that mean? Get to the net, not hit harder. When discussing doubles strategies, there is an old Australian saying: First to the net, first to the pub (to celebrate your win).

11. There are nine opportunities to get to the net.

   a. When receiving a short, mid-court-landing easy ball.

   b. When you hit a high topspin drive to buy time to approach.

   c. To take advantage of an opponent's pop-up shot by hitting a swing volley to approach.

   d. When you have successfully lobbed an opposing net player.

   e. When your partner at the net receives a short easy lob from your opponent and is about to hit an overhead.

   f. When you receive an easy, no pressure, soft second serve.

   g. When you decide to serve and volley.

   h. When one of your opponents is positioned mid-court, drop your shot at their feet and approach.

   i. When your opponent runs to the net to reach a short ball, you should also run to the net.

12. Things to try if you are losing badly or if you are expected to lose.

    a. Both play from the baseline. This will make it more difficult for your opponents to aggressively hit winning shots or get open court opportunities.

    b. Play brave and hit aggressively down the middle between your opponents.

    c. Lob a lot to force your opponents to hit tough deep overheads.

WHERE DO THESE FUZZY EGGS COME FROM?

d. Play more actively by approaching the net and poaching a lot; play more aggressively.

e. Play "Aussie" to force your opponents to return serves down the line.

13. Who takes the no-ad point?

 a. The most reliable returner.

 b. You can alternate with your partner—with a successful returner also taking the next one. Psych out your opponents by fighting over who wants it.

14. How to always hold your serve. When serving and volleying, get the first serve in, split step just before the service line, hit the first volley deep back to the receiver, and close in a little further. With both you and your partner positioned comfortably at the net, you will always (maybe more often than not) hold your serve.

15. Plan to hit all groundstrokes, approach shots, and volleys back to the deep opponent until you get an easy ball. Then your targets change:

 a. Angle off on the deep opponents' side.

 b. Hit down the middle, between your opponents.

 c. Hit through the opponents' "close player" at the net.

16. Never change a winning game plan. Always change a losing game plan. There are many ways of losing a match. You might as well try them all!

17. When both doubles teams are in a one up, one back situation and one of the net players is forced to switch, it is a very effective move for the other team to also switch. This will catch the original switching team by surprise.

On the following pages are diagrams for playing smart doubles. Here's the key to those diagrams:

The writing above the tennis court is the doubles tip.

- U – You
- P – Your Partner
- OA – Opponent – A
- OB – Opponent – B

❶ Keep ball going to the deep player
   1. Baseline
   2. Approach
   3. Volley

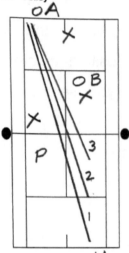

X = target for an easy ball

❷ Opponents both at the net targets
   1. Weaker player
   2. Down the Middle
   3. Lob

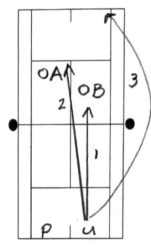

OB is weaker

❸ Playing more aggressively
   NO - hitting harder
   YES – getting to net

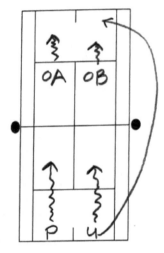

U hit a great lob

❹ Opponent OB is poaching a lot

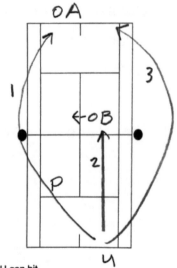

U can hit
   1. High drive CC to OA
   2. Fast ball at OB
   3. Lob over OB

❺ U poaches when the opportunity comes.

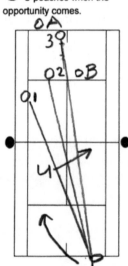

U has to watch where the ball lands
   1. No – watch the alley
   2. No – back up a little
   3. Yes – as soon as OA's head goes down to watch the ball

❻ Move as a team, P volleys wide

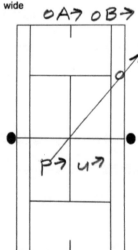

OB goes for shot
OA moves to middle
U watches alley
P covers down the middle and cross court

7 Easy ball
Pick a Target

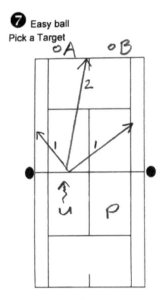

1. Angle off
2. Down the middle

8 Defending an easy overhead

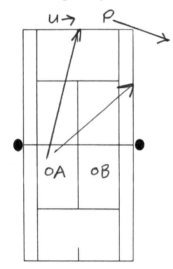

8 Defending an easy overhead

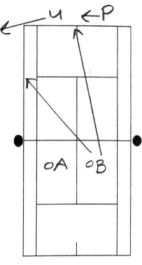

Give them the down the line (cover the middle and the wide cross court)

9 Don't have to break the ball

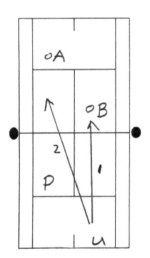

1. Speed ball
2. Hit a low drive and approach mid-court opponent OA. Partner P could poach.

1 0 Good players lob a lot. Don't be too predictable (mix in some lobs).

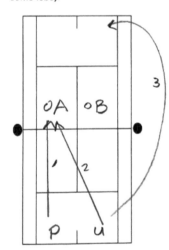

OA is weaker player.
1 & 2 drives.
3 lobs.
After a couple of drives, a lob is a good choice.

1 1 All 4 at the net. Pretend the ball is coming to you.

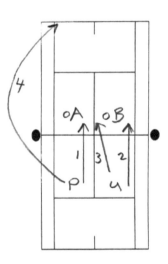

P1 Inside – Inside
U2 Outside – outside
3 Keep ball low, hit to OA (weaker player), speed at AO BO
4 Quick lob surprise

❶ ❷ Switching
Short ball, low bounce

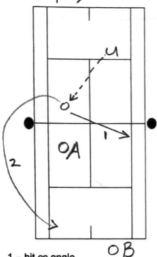

1 – hit cc angle
2 – Lob OA

❶ ❸ Switching
Short ball, high bounce

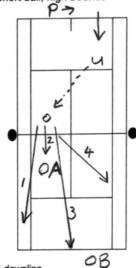

1 downline
2 through OA
3 down middle
4 angle cc

❶ ❹ When opponent lobs U

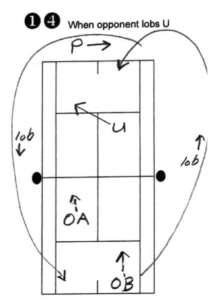

Lob a lob force O's to hit a tough smash
U calls switch, not P

❶ ❺ Net player U ever turn to watch partner's shot?

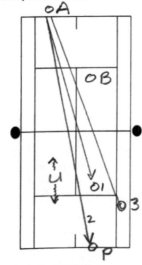

O1 No easy short ball
O2 Tough deep ball – Yes
O3 Tough wide ball – Yes
U moves towards the net when P drives and backs up a little when ball is hit to P

❶ ❻ Center court volley –
follow the ball

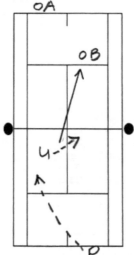

U volleys down on OB and follows the ball to keep pressure on OB

❶ ❼ Mostly serving targets

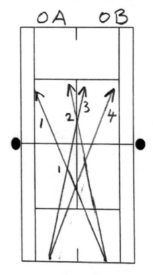

1 – No – can angle you cc
1 – No – Partner has to watch the alley
3 – No - Most like forehands
Mostly to 2 & 4 and between 3-4

9 Ways for You to Get to the Net

❶❽ #1 - Short ball

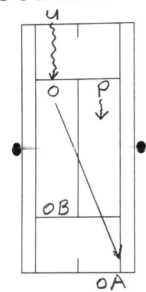

❶❾ #2 - High Drive

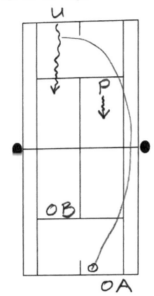

❷⓿ #3 - Swing Volley

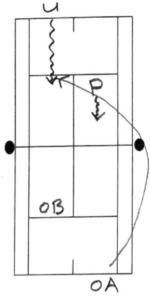

❷❶ #4 - Lob Opponent

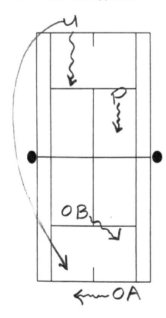

❷❷ #5 - Partner gets a short lob

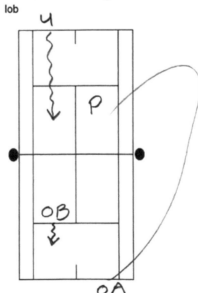

❷❸ #6 - Receiving a soft serve

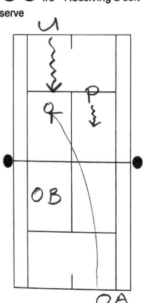

9 Ways for You to Get to the Net

❷❹ #7 - Serve and volley

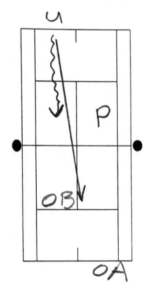

❷❺ #8 - At the feet of mid-court opponent

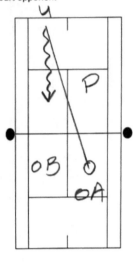

❷❻ #9 - If opponent is running up to reach a short ball

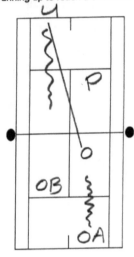

Some Approaches You Can Do at Any time (2, 4, 6, 7)

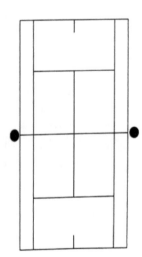

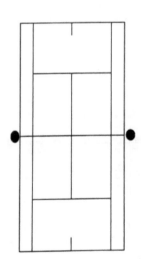

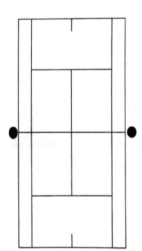

Play Aussie (Tandem)

❷❼ To force a great serve returner to change their target area:

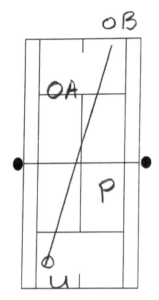

U serving
OB has great cc return

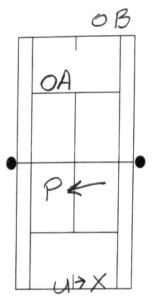

U after serving from the middle
crosses over to X

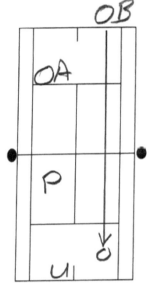

Your partner sets up at the net on
your side forcing OB to hit down
the line

❷❽ To hide a weakness on your team (your partner has a weak backhand)

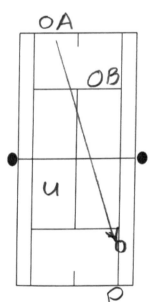

P serving to deuce side
P hits more forehands

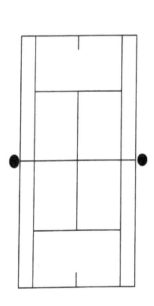

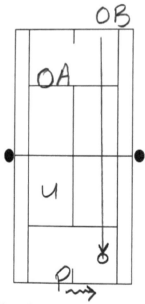

P serving to ad side by playing
Aussie, P will again hit more
forehands.

Who takes the ball down the middle? 5 Possibilities.

1

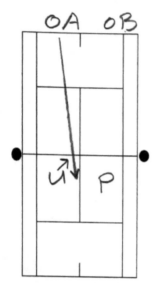

Forehand U do

2

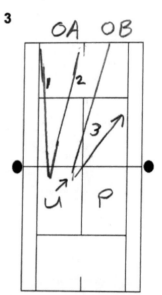

Player closer to the net can do more damage.

3

U have hit 2 shots in a row and now have the momentum so take the #3 hit coming down the middle.

4 Player playing the best

5 Best player

❸ ⓪ Relate to where the ball is…more so than where your opponents are!!!

1 Opponents chasing down a lob

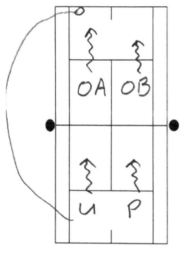

Are U in trouble? No. Anticipate a lob back.

2 U drop the ball low and close to the net

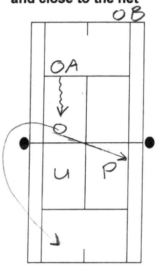

Are you in trouble? No. Anticipate OA going CC with an angle or lobbing (no power shot)

3 Your partner pops up a shot lob

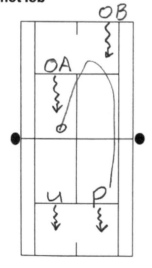

Are you in trouble? Yes. Anticipate backup up until OA is about to hit. OB moves up to net.

4 U hit a shot back to OA

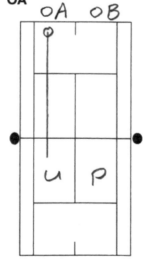

All players stay where they are.

5 U force OB to go wide

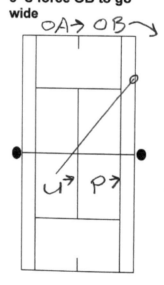

All players move in the direction of the ball.

POACHING

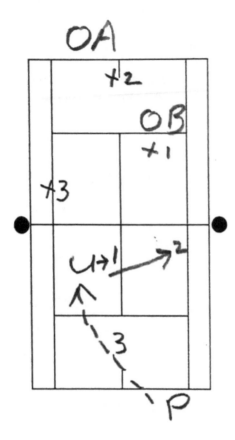

PICTURE U POACHING

Poaching is when a player moves across the net to intercept a ball heading toward their partner. The net player signals to their partner at the baseline.

    a) Closed fist – they are staying.

    b) Open hand means they are going to poach.

    c) Only index finger pointing means a head motion, fake poach (no poach).

From the diagram labled Poaching:

a) U → 1. A one-step poach, volley or overhead, stay, no poach.

b) U → 2. Run across the net to poach on your partner's side of the court, then stay on that side. Your partner, P, will cross behind you to cover the side you just left (line 3).

Your poaching targets are:

- X1 – At the feet and through OB.
- X2 – Down the middle of the court between OA and OB.
- X3 – Sharp angled on player OA's side.

I Formation

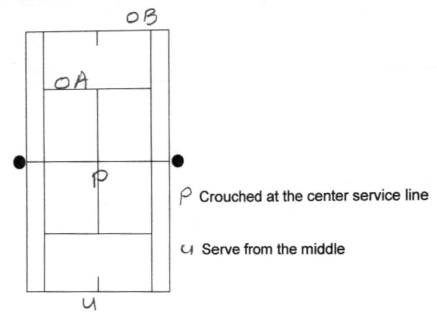

ρ Crouched at the center service line

$\mathfrak{u}$ Serve from the middle

a) Since the server is responsible for holding serve, they must be involved in the setup of the serve and net movement strategy.

b) Rather than giving hand signals, partners should talk and decide between points on where the service should go, according to any strengths and weaknesses of the opponents and the best strategies to do.

c) At the club level, the biggest advantage of using the I formation strategy is watching opponents freak out.

d) To some extent facing the I formation is a guessing game. Mixing in some fast drives down the middle of the court may not be a bad idea since the net player moves to either side.

e) The server and active net partner can take advantage of their strengths or known opponent weaknesses.

f) The I formation strategy will only work if the server's partner (crouched at the net) has the leg strength to get out of the crouched stance quickly and move off to either side.

2 Player Doubles Drills (no coach is involved in the drills)

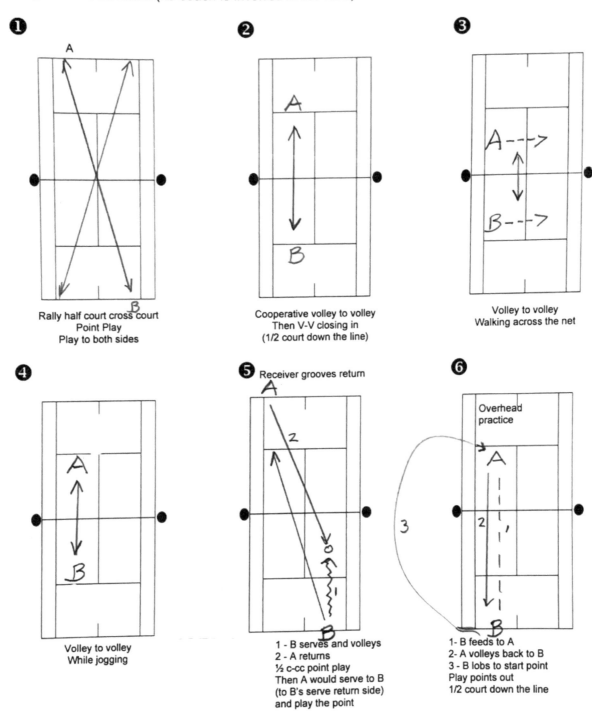

①

A

Rally half court cross court
Point Play
Play to both sides

B

②

A

B

Cooperative volley to volley
Then V-V closing in
(1/2 court down the line)

③

A - - ->

B - - ->

Volley to volley
Walking across the net

④

A

B

Volley to volley
While jogging

⑤ Receiver grooves return

A

2

B

1 - B serves and volleys
2 - A returns
½ c-cc point play
Then A would serve to B
(to B's serve return side)
and play the point

⑥

Overhead
practice

A

2

B

1- B feeds to A
2- A volleys back to B
3 - B lobs to start point
Play points out
1/2 court down the line

2 Player Doubles Drills
(a doubles team practicing)

❼

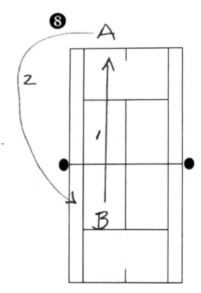

B practices midcourt strokes
Change spots, then change
sides

❽

Practicing lobs
1 - B feeds to A
2 - A lobs down the line
Play point out ½ court

❾

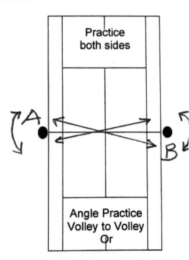

Practice
both sides

Angle Practice
Volley to Volley
Or

Hitting Groundstrokes

❿

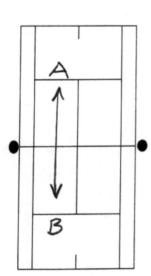

Volley to volley
Point Play
½ court down the line

⓫

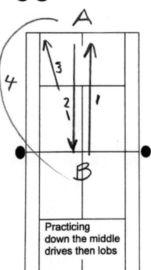

Practicing
down the middle
drives then lobs

1 - B feeds to A to start
2 - A drives at B (down the middle)
3 - B friendly volley to deuce side
4 - A lobs to start point
Then B would volley to Ad side

⓬ Playing a set returning
from their side

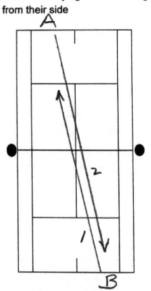

1 - B serves to A's side
Play games out half court cross
court
2 - A returns all shots cross court
A would then serve to B

Chapter 6

The Mental Game

KEEP YOUR HEAD; DON'T LOSE IT!

SOME THOUGHTS

1. The mind sets the body in motion; otherwise, the body simply goes through the motions.

a. Before serving the first serve, say quietly under your breath, "This ball is not coming back," and proceed to serve an ace.

b. Before serving a second serve, say quietly under your breath, "I am going to hurt my opponent so badly with this serve that they will make a mistake or give me a weak return."

2. You should not have to beat two players to win a singles match. If you have to work so hard to get yourself under control to play with your desired emotional mindset, you are competing against two opponents: yourself and your opponent. That's a tough match for you to win.

3. A spectator should have a tough time telling who is winning or losing. Be under mental and physical control.

4. Project the image of a tough competitor. Have a positive attitude and know what is happening around you: what the score is, when to change ends, the allowable time between points and changeovers; in short, the basic rules and game etiquette.

5. Most players tend to get down on themselves if things aren't going well. So, to be fair to yourself, take the time to build confidence. When you do something well, give yourself a verbal pat on the back. "Wow! I liked what I just did. I can play this game!"

6. Learn from your mistakes. Was it a technical error due to stroke execution? Should you have improvised your technique? Did you choose the right stroke? Did you make a bad decision? Or was it simply a great shot hit by your opponent? Make the analysis quickly, then clear your computer and move on to the next point.

7. Take the time to get pumped up and ready to play. I can remember my pre-competition ritual before competing in the various sports that I played during my high school years. I would walk, pacing back and forth, much like the tigers do in their cages in a zoo. My mother could always be heard saying, "I think Tilly is ready to compete." She was right!

8. You can occasionally yell out. As long as what you verbalize is positive, instructional, or motivational, that will send a message to your opponent that you have come to compete, not just play.

I'LL CLOBBER HER...I'LL CRUSH HER...I'LL SMASH HER...I'LL...I'LL...STICK MY TONGUE OUT AT HER!

9. Stick with your game plan, and don't give up on your plan too early. It may take a few games to see if your plan is working. Should you lose the first set 7-5, it may not be necessary to change your plan. If you lost the first set 6-0 and are down 2-0 in the second set, that would indicate you need to make a game plan adjustment.

10. It may be possible to trick yourself into getting into a match when a loss looks inevitable. I can remember a match that was very close, a real dogfight in the third set. I was down 5-2 with my opponent serving. I emotionally pictured myself losing and decided I had nothing to lose and hit out more aggressively. The momentum changed with my more aggressive hitting, and before I knew it, the score was tied 5-5 in the third set. I ended up winning the match 7-5 in the third set. I don't, however, recommend this strategy as being part of your strategic game plan!

"GULP"

11. If sticking to a particular game plan or staying focused for a long time is difficult (tennis matches can be long, drawn-out affairs), divide the match into smaller groups of games. Just set some goals for the next 3-4 games.

12. If you lose confidence, become more cautious, perhaps a little nervous, and that little voice inside your head is telling you to be more careful, tell that little voice to "shut up" and that you want to keep playing!

13. Play your matches at the pace you feel most comfortable—no rushing around be-

tween points; move with a confident stride! After a long rally, catch your breath and move a little slower. If winning, move along at a slightly faster pace. If losing, slow down the match pace a little. Take the full 20 seconds between points and the minute and a half at changeovers.

14. Fear of losing is a big killer. Who really cares how your match turns out? Perhaps only you, your coach, your family, and your close friends. I can be seen having a post-match drink with one of my students who just lost a match. It doesn't follow that a loser is a bad person and a winner is a good person. Think back, if you will, to a match you lost two years ago. You can hardly remember it, no one else can remember it, and they were there at the time. Who really cares about your match results? Who are you playing for? I'll give you a clue; it's not your coach, not your parents, or your friends. It's you! Play for yourself.

a. <u>A True Story</u>. In Melbourne in the spring of 1963, I played in the Victorian Junior Championships, open to juniors throughout Australia, and played on the grass courts at Kooyong. Playing good tennis and blessed with a little luck, I made it to the semifinals. I had played good tennis to beat John Cooper in three sets in the quarterfinals. I was a little lucky because Tony Roche pulled out of our scheduled third-round match with a twisted ankle. My opponent in the semifinals, Owen Davison, was a clear favorite to win the match, but I wanted to do well. I wanted to do more than just play; I wanted to compete. My dad took a sick day from work to come and watch the match. The Kooyong grass was never greener, the summer sky never bluer. It was a big deal. My name was on the scoreboard, and it was spelled right. I can remember being a little nervous before the match but relieved that the nervousness had disappeared after the first game. Owen held serve, I held serve, then Owen held serve. I was down 2-1 on serve and feeling good that I was in the match and competing. Then, I felt the bottom fall out of the match. It wasn't a cramp. It wasn't a migraine. It was my emotional reaction to seeing the legendary

Australian great, Frank Sedgman, take a seat in the first row of the spectator stands. I tightened up; after all, the great Frank Sedgman was watching me. My game went downhill. While I tightened up, Owen played well. I never won another game (losing, 6-1, 6-0). I was bitterly disappointed that I wasn't able to compete. An hour after the match, while sitting in the clubhouse lounge, Frank Sedgman came by again. He noticed me sitting by the window and stopped to ask if I'd played yet. My mouth dropped! It didn't take me long to figure out what had happened. Frank had simply sat down alongside our court to chat with a friend, not really paying attention to who was playing. I thought he'd been watching me. I had been playing for him! After Frank's arrival, my shoulders and my mind tightened because I thought he'd been watching me play. I psychologically walked out of the match because of my reaction to him. Indirectly, I had played the match for him. I played for the wrong person. I realized the only person I should play for is myself.

15. Have a good, competitive attitude, try very hard to win, but link success with

DON'T LISTEN TO THAT LITTLE DEVIL, MR. NEGATIVE ATTITUDE!

hustling and playing smart— not winning and losing. I tell my students that I have never lost a match in my life-- according to the score I have—but I always walk off the court feeling like a winner because of my effort. I tell my students that if they try very hard, hustle, play smart, have a good attitude and good sportsmanship, they too can walk off the court following a lost match with their heads held up! It is possible to lose a match if your opponent plays better than you. Can you feel a little disappointed and down in the dumps? Yes, that means you care. But let feelings last for about 20 minutes, then evaluate your match, learn from it, and then clear your computer, move ahead, and look forward to your next appointment with a tennis court.

16. After matches, evaluate your effort. What worked well? What didn't work? What needs work? Set new goals to help you improve.

17. Arrange a variety of practice matches.

    a. Players not quite as good as you (so you can push them around and practice your game plan)

    b. Players close to your ability (so you can gain match play experience that can help you win matches)

    c. Players better than you (so you can experience working hard just to win some points and have a vision of where you are, hopefully, heading)

PICK YOUR NEXT OPPONENT... CHECK ONE!

18. Have something enjoyable to do post-match and look forward to doing it, win or lose.

19. Surround yourself with happy, positive, supportive, friendly, and loyal people.

20. Remember how you feel following a match win compared to how you feel following a match loss. It will motivate you to play better in your matches.

21. Develop a positive attitude. Being "well whispered" helps. That means someone must feed you encouraging, flattering, complimentary support. Someone must tell you that you are good.

   a. Tell yourself when you feel deserving.

   b. Your coach can pump you up when deserving.

   c. Your parents and friends can shower you with compliments and encouragement when you deserve it.

   d. You have arrived when you believe that you are deserving. Any compliments must be deserving. The receiver of the compliments must believe that the compliments are true and not just made-up verbiage.

22. A winning formula is $P + E = R$.

   P = Preparation

   E = Effort

   R = Result

   Take care of the P and E. The R will take care of itself.

23. Forget things in the periphery, how many spectators are watching, what if I lose, etc.

24. Most matches will have momentum changes. If losing badly, slow down the pace of the match, mix up your shots, mostly drive, mix in high deep topspin drives, and, occasionally, short, sliding, short-angled shots. If on a roll and you are winning, keep the pace of the match going. Make things happen. Go for it!

25. Take nothing for granted. Respect all opponents. Assume that your opponents have the ability to beat you, but you still keep a confident "can win" attitude and your game plan of controlled aggressiveness going.

26. When setting up for a shot, decide what to hit and then execute your planned shot.

27. Value the reputation of being a fighter, a player who hustles and never gives up or emotionally walks out of a match.

28. Try not to be outwardly, obnoxiously confident. Be inwardly cocky and believe in yourself.

29. Never change a winning game plan. Always change a losing game plan. There are many ways to lose a tennis match. You may as well try them all!

30. You can! Life is not a rehearsal.

31. Try to understand the game; feel the game. Develop many "natural tactical reactions" that help you be more efficient in winning points. Don't simply learn things by heart.

32. The world remembers the gold medal winners and competitors that hustle. It's easier to hustle!

33. Coach yourself through positive self-talk (I can and I will).

34. Most coaches in most sports will tell you that "Games are won on the practice court; you can't get serious the day of the game."

TAKE UP THE CHALLENGE TO HANDLE ADVERSITY

Dictionaries define adversity as "Finding yourself in unfavorable circumstances; unhappy conditions."

In common, everyday language, it means that someone or something is ripping on you, and you don't like what's happening. Adversity occurs in both everyday living and on the tennis court. You can transfer the experiences you have learned to handle in one area to help overcome some difficulties you are encountering in other areas. When adversity rears its ugly head, you have choices to handle the situation. One is to emotionally and physically disappear, just walk away as if it wasn't happening (easy way out). Another is to commit to trying to better handle the situation. Let's go with the second option.

WIGLEY NEVER COULD HANDLE ADVERSITY!

SOME THOUGHTS ON HANDLING SPECIFIC ADVERSITIES

1. <u>You are getting bad line calls.</u>

After the first bad call, you could calmly ask your opponent, "Are you sure?" If the call happens again, for a second time, during a break in play, you could find the person running the tournament and say, "We are having trouble with the line calls and would appreciate a line judge be assigned to our court." A very tactful plea for help instead of "That little schnick down the other end is cheating me." That could start a coach and/or parent riot. Ideally, an adult could be assigned to monitor any call problems. Before play continues, the monitoring rules should be discussed. Players will continue to call their own lines, but if a disagreement occurs, the assigned line watcher should be consulted. The line watcher should not be expected to call all the lines.

a. Some thoughts on player line calling:

a) If your opponent's shot looks like it will definitely be in or definitely out, there should be no need to overdo watching where the ball lands. However, if you feel the incoming ball will be a difficult call, really open your eyes wide and focus on getting the decision right.

b) The tennis rule book does recognize a situation where a player may ask their opponent for help with a line call. If you are up at the net and your opponent hits a passing shot that you are not able to see land (considering the sideline), you may ask your opponent for help with the call. If you ask, you must go with the opponent's call. If they are not able to call, then the ball must be called in.

c) If the incoming shot lands close to the line and you are not 100% sure it was out, the ball may have touched the line. You cannot make the call. You must call it in.

d) On a close call, you can make that shot and then immediately call the ball out if, in fact, it was out. It is easy to see how calling your own half of the court could lead to some problems. Imagine a baseball game where the batter calls balls or strikes. Are you kidding me?!

2. <u>You are playing a pusher.</u>

There is an old Australian tennis saying: "Show me a pusher, and I will show you a room full of trophies." The pusher gives you nothing. Their attitude is, *I'm not going to mess up. If you want to win a point, you will have to hit some great shots.* A true pusher plays like a scrooge! Pushers feel more comfortable at the baseline. They are human backboards. A true pusher will visibly turn pale once they cross the service line.

a. If you push against a pusher, you lose 6-1, 6-2.

b. If you try to hit a lot of quick winners, you lose 6-2, 6-1.

c. If you approach the net at an opportune time, you may have to hit three or four good shots to win a point (a good groundstroke, approach shot, volley, overhead), you lose 6-3, 6-4.

d. If you mix up pulling the pusher to the net and you coming to the net at an opportune time, you win the first set 7-5, lose the second set 6-4, and lose the third set in a tiebreaker 7-6. You still lose, but at least your score will look better on the draw sheet!

Seriously! Here are some ideas on beating a pusher:

A. Pull the pusher off the court to earn an open court shot:
    1. Immediately when serving
        i. Slice serve to the deuce side.
        ii. Kick serve to the ad side.
    2. Cut the pusher's sideline when you receive an easy wide ball (three chances of winning)
        i. They cannot get to your shot.
        ii. They struggle to get to your shot and make an error.
        iii. They get your shot back over the net but have left the whole court open for you to hit a winning shot.
B. Pull the pusher to the net by hitting a cheap drop shot (the idea is to pull the pusher to the net, not to win the point with the drop shot):
    1. Immediately when you receive an easy second serve.
    2. Rally long enough to get an easy mid-court ball.
C. Hit an approach shot off the same easy mid-court ball. You can also hit a drop shot.
    1. Hit a deep, semi-lob, heavy topspin drive (to the pusher's weak side).
    2. Hit a swing volley approach shot.

D. Mix up your shots to take the pusher out of their rhythm. Mostly drive, mix in short sliders, mix in deep, high-bouncing, topspin drives.

E. Rather than go for an amazing winner, you may have to hit two winning shots to win the point.

WORDS OF WISDOM

Note: Avoid the long baseline to baseline rallies. That is *their* game. Take the pusher out of the baseline to baseline rallying. Force the pusher to receive passing shots or have to hit passing shots.

OH-OH! ... I THINK I HAVE TO GO!!!

The bottom line is that your strategies are to create open court shots, pull them in, you come in, mix up shots. Would you rather hit passing shots or volleys or overheads? Choose what is working best.

3. <u>Crowd clapping only for your opponent.</u>

This may happen when playing on the opposing player's home court. Say there are 20 people watching your match. They are friends of your opponent. Remember, they don't hate you; they would just prefer their friend to win the match. Think: this could be the biggest win in your life, beating 21 people in one match (one opponent and 20 spectators). Imagine calling and saying, "Mom, I beat 21 people today. Yes, 21, one player and 20 of their friends cheering for my opponent." Your mother replies, "Wow! Great job, dear!" Take up the challenge. Don't take the easy way out by telling yourself, "Life's cruel. I can't believe this is happening to me," and then emotionally and physically walking out of the match.

4. Too many people watching.

Not everyone likes to play on court 1 in front of hundreds of spectators. Some players would like this scenario. Don't think you are on a pedestal being analyzed. No one should affect the way you play. Let's take a tongue-in-cheek look at the 100-person crowd:

a. You are a better player than 70 of the watchers. They shouldn't affect the way you play.

b. Twenty members of the crowd are not nice people. They come home from work, kick the dog, and yell at the wife. They should not affect the way you play.

c. I remember from health education classes at the University of Oregon that ten percent of the population are nose pickers. That takes care of the last ten spectators.

No one watching should affect the way you play.

5. Playing a big hitter.

Now and again, they will give you a point. I love to play someone who gives free points. Make them hit a lot of balls and lengthy rallies. Aim more shots to their weaker side. Mix up your shots to keep the ball out of their comfortable hitting area, particularly:

a. Hit heavy, high-bouncing topspin shots.

b. Hit short wide sliders.

They may still try to hit aggressively even if they are uncomfortable. Force them to improvise often so they cannot hit as many comfortable, aggressive shots. Really hustle to force them to hit two to three winning shots to win the point.

6. **If you are making too many errors.**

a. Are you trying for too much speed and not enough control? Remember, speed by itself is useless. Put something on the end of speed:

a) Speed with feeling

b) Speed with a little spin

c) Speed with placement

b. Be prepared to improvise if you don't have time to set up for a comfortable shot.

c. Analyze your errors to see if shot selection could be a problem.

d. When you get an easy ball, take your time and pick a target. That will give your put away shot more purpose.

e. Check your emotional level. Perhaps you are rushing your shots.

7. **Your opponent is hitting too many winners.**

Perhaps you are not doing enough. Increase your rally speed. Hit your drives higher over the net so that your shots land deeper. Mix up your shots—a few faster drives, a few high, deep drives; throw in a few short, wide slices. Give your opponent a different look by mixing in some approach shots. Given an opportunity, cut the sides lines to pull your opponent off the court. Reevaluate your opponent's weaknesses.

8. **Your opponent is running around backhands, ripping forehands.**

The goal would be to get the ball to their backhand side.

a. Serve a heavy slice serve to the deuce side to open up the backhand target for a winning shot or an approach shot.

b. During a rally, when receiving a wide comfortable forehand, cut the sideline to open up their backhand target.

c. Hit an angle forehand cross court. Chances are it will be open.

d. Serve immediately to your opponent's backhand. Use a little wider serve position when serving to the ad side, and use a kick serve to target the backhand.

e. You may have to hit a faster, wider, or shorter drive to your opponent's backhand side so he has a more difficult time running around it.

GOTCHA !

9. Gamesmanship

Your opponent is trying to psych you out, to rattle you, to make you feel bad, to make you feel inadequate, to make you angry, to distrust yourself. Recognize what is happening. Don't play their game and retaliate. Channel your emotions towards a determined effort to beat them. The following gamesmanship examples are true. Only the names have been changed to protect the innocent.

a. <u>Jane lost her match on the car ride to her match</u>. More often than not, large junior tournaments have many different venues like extra high school courts, park and recreation facilities, etc. On this particular day, Jane and her opponent got a ride to one of these off-tournament sites. Jane's opponent was a talker. "I play at a tennis academy for a couple of hours four times a week." Jane was verbally jolted to pay attention. "I have won the last three tournaments I've played in," her opponent continued. By the time the car reached the match courts, Jane had been brainwashed into believing there was no way she could compete with this girl. Jane hustled and played her hardest but fell short emotionally and lost. Her opponent had gotten into her head. We talked at length about this experience during our next tennis lesson. Jane understood what happened, and her last comment to me was, "I'm never falling for that trick again."

b. <u>Jon lost on the side of the court while getting ready to warm up</u>. Jon and his opponent sat on a courtside bench and readied themselves for their tournament match. Jon took his racquet, water bottle, and towel out of his bag and was ready to play. His opponent moved in slow motion and seemed to be purposely putting on a show for Jon. An obvious "watch what I've got" boastful exhibition of intimidation, taking four racquets out of his tennis bag, one at a time, to check their tension and then dropping them in a pile by his side. He selected one and returned the other three to his tennis bag. He then took out an extra-long bright yellow sweatband from his bag and slowly positioned it on his left wrist. And then he pulled out a bright green sweatband to put on his right wrist. I looked at Jon and could not help but notice he had a look of "I'm not sure I can beat this kid" on his face. His opponent was putting on a show, and, unfortunately, Jon was taking his opponent's display too seriously. He became psychologically deflated. He was intimidated, which may have contributed to his less-than-best performance. He was eventually defeated. Were his opponent's actions gamesmanship? It did look like it!

c. <u>Brent may have lost his match at the end of the second set</u>. Brent was playing well and having a tough battle with a very competitive, good opponent in a boys 16's junior tournament. Brent won the first set 6-4 but was down 2-5 in the second set. As the players changed ends, Brent's opponent asked him a question. "If we split sets, do we play a super tiebreaker, or do we play out the third set?" Brent took issue with that question and rebuttal with, "Let's wait and see who wins the second set." He was visibly affected by his opponent's premature questions and did not play well to finish the match. As it turned out, Brent lost the second set 6-4 and the super tiebreaker 10-7 to decide the match.

d. <u>Robert's opponent attempted an unbelievably mean strategy to try to upset his concentration in their close third set</u>. The match was on serve, with the score 4-3 in the third set. The players were just starting to change ends of the court. Robert's opponent was walking along the baseline, about to walk to the other end of the court. Walking, he dripped water from his water bottle along the baseline Robert was about to play on for the next two games. Are you kidding me!? No! Luckily, Robert's coach saw what was happening and quickly raced off to file a complaint with the tournament director. The tournament director saw what had happened and ordered Robert's opponent to get an old towel from the club pantry and soak up the water before they could resume the match. Robert won the third set 7-5 and, in my humble opinion, deserved to win.

10. <u>What can you possibly do if you lose your backhand?</u>

$2,000 worth of tennis lessons on your backhand is down the drain.

a. If there's time and you are fast enough, run around your backhand to hit a forehand.

b. Take a stance to show your opponent a 60% forehand target and a 40% backhand target.

c. Slice or block your backhand deep down the middle of the court (more of a defensive hang-in-there shot) and be more aggressive with your forehand.

I had a student use the above strategies once due to his left lower arm injury. It was put in a cast. He barely tried to play for his high school. His cast made it difficult for him to effectively use his two-handed backhand. The story has a great ending as he battled through this adversity to win the state high school singles final.

11. <u>You are supposed to lose the match.</u>

Your opponent is too good for you. You're overmatched. Here are some things you can try:

a. Play brave. You have the green light to hit the ball. Serve more aggressively.

b. When you get an easy ball or an open court, go for a winner.

c. Ask yourself a question, "Do I feel more comfortable finishing points at the net or hitting pass shots?" Do what you do best.

d. Mix up your shots, hit some rally speed drives, some high, deep, landing topspin drives, and some short, angled sliders. Hopefully, you'll be taking your opponent out of their rhythm by *not* feeding them comfortable balls.

It's quite possible your opponent is not at their best.

    a. They had a recent fight with their partner the night before the match.

    b. They got a D on their chemistry exam.

    c. They ate an extra spicy Chinese meal.

    d. They didn't get enough sleep.

    e. They notice that you're short and chubby and take you for granted.

You have nothing to lose. You start out strong, and you're up 3-1. They tighten up! You are in the match!

12. <u>Playing in extreme heat.</u>

a. Have a good mental attitude. Be determined to handle it. The first person that says, "It's' too hot today; I'd rather be in a cool movie theater," loses.

b. Dress white and light, be smart, wear a hat, use sunscreen, have a towel, and loosely tie a wet bandana around your neck.

c. Take the 20-second break between points and the 1.5 minutes at changeovers to rest or stand in the shade.

d. Make your opponent move, corner to corner hitting two deep balls followed by a short slider.

e. If you're getting tired, shorten the point by hitting more winners, approaching the net, and drop-shot your opponent.

f. Adjust your ball lift or position along the baseline to avoid looking into the sun when serving.

g. Lob high to your opponent in situations where they have to look into the sun.

h. Have some snacks in your tennis bag for quick energy.

i. Hydrate the night before your match, and drink plenty of water during your match.

j. Drink a sports drink to get electrolytes.

k. Save energy by walking between points and spend as much time in the shade as possible.

l. Having a small, cool, wet towel to wipe your face and neck at changeovers will help you feel better. You must also have a dry towel ready to dry your hands so you can hold your racquet.

13. **Playing in high wind conditions.**

Plan to make the wind your friend. Find a fluttering flag or use some other technique to figure out which way the wind is blowing.

A. Playing with the wind

Playing with the wind, you can come to the net more confidently. Be careful not to overhit drives and use topspin more often to dip the ball. Drop shots are not as effective. With the wind at your back, lobs may go long, so you should lob carefully. If your opponent drops a ball short, it's not going to come through, so you should run up on short balls. A serve and volley strategy works particularly well with the wind at your back. A serve that pulls your opponent off the court is very effective. Generally, play from a court position one step *inside* the baseline.

B. Playing against the wind

Now you can hit drives harder, but it's more difficult to approach the net confidently. In this situation, both drop shots and aggressively hit lobs are very effective shots. Slice shots will sit up. When serving, try to pull the opponent off the court on the deuce side. The wind will help this serve. Generally, play from a court position one step *behind* the baseline.

Here are some general tips for playing in a high wind:

a. Accentuate your footwork since the ball path may change unpredictably in the last fraction of a second. Prepare mentally to make a quick adjustment when organizing the body just prior to ball contact.

b. Hit solid, decisive strokes so that the wind is less likely to take control of the ball.

c. When serving, lift the ball a little lower on the serve and hit the serve with a shortened or faster loop. This adjustment in technique will restrict the ball from being blown away.

d. When playing in an "across the court" wind situation, take the time to figure out what your stroke emphasis should be when hitting either down the line or cross court. You may need a little less speed or more control when hitting in one direction and possibly choose to hit more aggressively with more speed when hitting in another direction. The first player to say, "I can't win today; it's too windy," will lose.

Figure out which way the wind is blowing and make the necessary court positioning, technique and strategy adjustments so that the *wind is your friend!*

"A man who will not be beaten cannot be beaten."

If you think you are beaten, you are.

If you think you dare not, you don't.

If you'd like to win but think you can't.

It's almost a cinch you won't.

If you think you'll lose, you're lost.

For out in the world you'll find

Success begins with a fellow's will

It's all in the state of mind.

If you think you're outclassed, you are.

We've got to think high to rise.

You've got to be sure of yourself before

You can ever win a prize.

Life's battles don't always go

To the stronger or faster man.

But sooner or later the man who wins,

Is the man who thinks he can.

--- Walter D. Wintle

(You can re-read this poem by replacing masculine pronouns with feminine pronouns.)

Chapter 7

Off-Court Tips That Can Help Improve On-Court Performance

(This section was written in collaboration with Mike Devenney, Chair of the Health Department and Tennis Coach at LaSalle Catholic College Prep High School (retired), Portland, Oregon, three-time Oregon State Athletic Association's Tennis Coach of the Year, Presenter at the 2000 USTA Tennis Teachers Conference.)

1. <u>Hydration</u>

    a. I remember watching a tennis match last summer where two young boys were locked at two games all in the third set. The weather was quite hot, and after one and a quarter hours of grueling tennis, one of the boys suddenly realized he was thirsty and began calling for his mother to get him some water. I thought to myself, *It's too late. Any water the boy may drink now will take over half an hour to be in usable form. The water he drinks now is not going to help him in this match.*

    b. Being properly hydrated is very important for performance. The best sports drink is water. It makes everything else in your body work better. It helps blood flow, cools your system, and carries away waste products. Water helps your muscles move smoother, your eyes see clearer, and your brain work sharper. Players should drink six to eight glasses of water per day and more if you're playing. A part of your match preparation ritual should be to drink plenty of water the evening before a tournament. Drink a few glasses of water on match morning, visit the restroom just before match time, and then sip water regularly during changeovers.

c. What you drink before a match will help you in the first set, what you drink in the first set will help you in the second set, and what you drink in the third set will help you feel better during the ride home.

d. To be sure that you are hydrated, check the color of your urine. If it's clear or a very pale yellow, you are in good shape. Darker colors are signs of dehydration. Sports drinks are engineered to help you maintain proper hydration during exercise and provide the body with essential electrolytes. Start drinking your sports drink 30-40 minutes before match time. It takes 15-20 minutes before the drink is turned into usable energy. Some brands of sports drinks may upset your digestive system, so experiment during practice sessions to confirm they are acceptable. It could spell curtains for you if you find out at 5-5 in the third set that your sports drink does not agree with you!

2. <u>Breakfast</u>

a. Breakfast is the most important meal of the day!

b. If you only want to play in the first round of a tournament, skip breakfast. A body needs energy. Do the math. If you eat dinner (let's say fish and chips with coleslaw on the side) at 6 pm and have a small snack at 10 pm just before going to bed, and then you skipped breakfast to get ten extra minutes of sleep before your 10 am first-round match, you just went 16 hours with very little for your body to feed on. Do *not* trade breakfast for an extra ten minutes of sleep! You may be a little more awake but unable to run down your opponent's drop shot.

c. Breakfast doesn't have to be three eggs, toast, and orange juice. Just about anything will do, even cold, leftover pizza (not recommending that, but it's better than nothing). The candy bar that you eat as you walk out for your first match of the day won't even come close to helping you out for another 45 minutes.

3. Sleep

   a. If you work hard on the practice courts and give it your all in matches, you need time to heal and get strong.

   b. The body repairs itself while it sleeps. Exercised muscles become stronger during sleep. And it has to be good sleep! Eight hours a night, every night of the week, and it doesn't work if you skimp on sleep during the week and try to catch up on the weekend.

   c. The sleep you get the night before a match is important, but the sleep you get the preceding two nights is more important. The energy stored two nights ago is what you will use in your match.

4. Diet

   a. Eat a well-balanced diet. This means grains, fruits, vegetables, meat, fish, and some dairy (or substitutes if you are allergic to dairy products). Eating close to nature is important. For example, an orange is better than orange juice.

   b. When you are scheduling your pre-match, between-match, and post-match meals, it is valuable to remember the following approximate digestion times:

      i. Large meal – 5 hours

      ii. Small meal – 2 hours

      iii. Liquid meal – 1 hour

      iv. Snack or sports drink – 1 hour

   c. Remember: supplements such as vitamins are meant to be used along with and not instead of real food.

5. <u>Match Meals</u>

   a. Pre-Match Meal

      i. When? 1.5-2 hours before your match.

      ii. What? Food high in carbohydrates that can be quickly and easily digested, such as potatoes, pasta, rice, and veggies.

      iii. Important: my high school health teacher explained why it's not smart to compete in a sport immediately following a large meal. To quote my teacher: "The blood cannot effectively take care of your digestive needs as well as your physical exertion needs. The blood has a tough time being in two places at the same time."

   b. Between-Match Meals

      i. Congratulations! You have won your first-round match. Now what?

      ii. Eating between matches can be tricky because one never knows the exact time of the next match. It is probably better for you to return to the court a little hungry rather than a little stuffed.

      iii. It is wise to eat foods that are easy to digest. Energy-rich snacks that are low in fat and high in carbohydrates are ideal. For example, simple breads such as bagels or pretzels and fruits such as bananas and oranges. Only eat foods you know. A between-match meal is no time to try Grandma's tuna fish surprise!

c. Post-Match Meals

    i. When? You have a 20-minute - two-hour window to replenish your nutritional needs.

    ii. What? Now you can have a more balanced blend of proteins, fats, and carbohydrates.

    iii. I was extremely happy to learn that some of my favorite foods were on the recommended post-match foods list, including string cheese, chocolate milk, and ice cream!

6. <u>Match Details and What to Take Out</u> on <u>the Court</u>

    a. It really helps if you make a "must bring" and a "must do" list when preparing to play a tournament.

        i. Pack your tennis bag the night before. It's a trap for players to leave preparation to the last minute.

        ii. Know the name of the tournament, where it's being played, directions to the site, and how you will get there.

        iii. Check in to the tournament site early, and familiarize yourself with the playing environment, type of courts, surrounding facilities (spectator stands, swimming pools, snack bars, etc).

        iv. Check in with the tournament desk early.

I GUESS I HAVE EVERYTHING!

v. Remember the match time and your opponent's name.

vi. Find a quiet, suitable place to warm up and stretch out.

vii. Doublecheck your carry-on tennis bag, have at least three racquets, a filled water bottle, sunscreen, hat, towel, Band-Aids, headache tablets, some clean clothes, especially dry socks, between-match snacks, etc.

b. I can remember helping 11-year-old Steven Finnigan prepare a list of "must bring" to his first national tournament. I underlined three racquets on his list and emphasized to him the importance of having three, just in case he breaks strings or misplaces a racquet. The day before flying to Dallas, Texas, for the tournament, Steven asked me if I had any of his brand and size racquets in stock. He wanted to take three more racquets to Dallas. I asked him why since he already had three racquets he liked. He hesitated and simply gave me the "fisheye." After a moment's silence, he quietly answered, "Just in case I play a seeded player." Fair enough!

7. Don't Play Hurt

a. Unless there are more than 100 spectators in the stands or your girlfriend/ boyfriend is watching the match (just kidding), you should not play hurt.

b. Players who play hurt lose a lot. Remember that pain is a sign that some-

IT ONLY HURTS WHEN I COME BACK TO DEUCE!

thing is wrong. Pay attention to what your body is telling you. Playing hurt may lead to serious injury and the need for extended recovery time.

c. Taking time off to rest, heal, and do therapy if needed is important. Rest is often the best treatment for both chronic and acute injuries.

d. Time off the court doesn't have to be wasted. Check with your doctor or physiotherapist for some cross-training possibilities.

e. Depending on the injury, activities such as running in water, biking, swimming, or walking could help your recovery.

8. Aftor tho Match

a. Take time to analyze the match.

b. What worked well for you?

c. What do you feel you need to work on?

d. Did you get overtired physically?

e. How did your strategies work?

f. Could you have done something differently?

g. What did you learn about your opponent?

h. Notes:

i. Put on dry socks and sandals after every match to give your feet a comfortable rest.

ii. Go into the next round with renewed confidence and a fresh pair of socks.

iii. Commit to taking good care of your body and health.

iv. Commit to working on improving your tennis, both mentally and physically.

v. Remind yourself that you get out of something exactly what you put into it!

Chapter 8

Warmup and Physical Fitness

A tennis player serious about preparing to play tournaments has to be full bottle or competent in four areas to have a chance to enjoy and have success when playing tennis.

1. Develop mechanically sound strokes. They are the tools that do the work.

2. Learn some smart strategies. Things to do to win points and make life miserable for your opponent.

3.Be mentally tough. Be emotionally under control, believe in your abilities, and handle adversity.

4. Be physically fit. So that you can hustle and hit the same solid strokes at the end of a long match as you hit in the first few games.

Some thoughts on warmup and dynamic stretching

1. Warmup activities should start out with a combination of moderate-intensity walking with intermittent light stretching exercises to gradually move towards more vigorous activity. In other words, a slow increase in physical exertion.

2. Start with a slow jog around the tennis court with your racquet in hand, bouncing a tennis ball on the court as you go. Slow down, or actually stop, to stretch while moving around the court. Remember to totally stop to do the stretches you are not able to perform while walking.

3. Then move onto the court for a stroke warmup. Again, with an emphasis on moderate intensity, moving to more vigorous activity.

4. It is important to remember to take some time to cool down after playing and include some light stretching. For example:

    a. 4-5 minutes of gentle jogging

    b. Stretching the main muscles used during the workout.

5. It is a trap for players to think that playing basketball or warming up in a jacuzzi is a good idea between matches. Rest, move into the shade, hydrate, reach for an energy bar, and focus on your game plan for the upcoming match.

LAST CALL FOR MR. ROONEY, ON CENTER
COURT PLEASE, MR. ROONEY?......MR. ROONEY?

This information on warmup and stretching is provided courtesy of Kurt Lindner, Head Boys Coach, Aloha High School, 6A Boys Tennis representative to the Oregon Athletic Coaches Association and 6A State Seeding Chairman to the Oregon School Activities Association, seven-time Metro League Coach of the Year, 2017 Section 8 High School Tennis Coach of the Year (AK, WA, OR, ID).

WARM UP AND STRETCHING (IF ONLY A SHORT PERIOD OF TIME IS AVAILABLE BEFORE HAVING TO START PLAY)

The best way to avoid this situation is to make it a point to get to every scheduled match at least an hour before you expect to play. You can soak up the atmosphere, get the feel of the facility, scout a possible opponent, and watch some tennis. That's if we lived in a perfect world. We don't. Sometimes things happen, and you arrive late to your play site. An effective warmup will increase your chances of better play; it's that simple. You want to make sure you are working all parts of the body—neck, shoulders, torso, fingers, wrists, hip flexors, knees, ankles, etc. This also includes many muscle groups—abs, quads, glutes, biceps, triceps, lats, calf muscles, etc.

I recommend dynamic stretching over static stretching before play. Dynamic stretching is stretching your muscles and joints while moving. Static stretching is staying stationary and not moving while holding your stretch for a short amount of time. There are tons of dynamic stretching movements that most people know, but it's best to focus on dynamic stretching that is specific to tennis. Do 3-5 minutes of moving in the form of jogging, skipping, side slides, or grapevines. Other dynamic stretching movements like hug lunges, squats, palm kicks, step-over hurdles forward and backward, burpees, and pushups will get your body ready for play. Find a safe spot and do 25-30 full-range shadow swings of each shot. Forehands, backhands, volleys, and serves. Find some open space inside or outside the facility that will allow you to do some of the things mentioned above.

EXERCISE DESCRIPTIONS: Palm Kicks, Side Slides, Grapevines, Burpees, Full Range Squats, Hug Lunges, Step Over Hurdles

PALM KICKS

Aim to extend one leg straight out in front of you as high as you can or to where your flexibility allows. Have your arms straight out in front of you. Raise one leg as high as you can to touch the opposite palm of one hand. Walk forward and repeat these motions on the other side. Keep your chest up and maintain a tall posture through-out the drill. It's also known as the "walking toe touch."

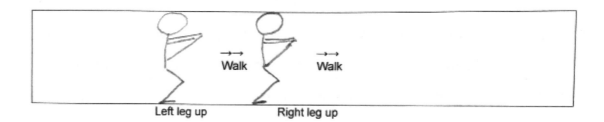
Left leg up   Right leg up

SIDE SLIDES

With knees bent and your weight on the balls of your feet, hop sideways without crossing your feet until your feet come close together. Repeat the process as you slide sideways, using your arms for balance.

Feet come closer together as you move along

GRAPEVINES

Begin by standing with your feet together. Be sure you have plenty of space, enough to allow you to make four big steps to your right. The grapevine is a lateral movement, so you will move to the right and back to the left. Step your right foot out to the right so that your feet are a little wider than hip-width apart. Pick up your left foot and step behind your right foot so that your legs are crossed in this position with your right foot in front and your left foot behind it. Step your right foot to the right again, uncrossing your stance. Bring your left foot to meet your right foot so that you are in the starting position. Now repeat the move to the left, leading with your left foot.

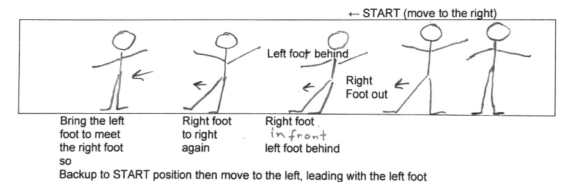

BURPEES

Standing tall, start the exercise by going into a squat position with your knees bent, back straight, and your feet about shoulder-width apart. Lower the palms of your hands to the floor in front of you so they're just inside your feet. With your weight on your hands, kick your feet back so you're on your hands and toes and in a pushup position. Keeping your body straight from head to heels, remember not to let your back sag or to stick your butt in the air. Do a frog kick by jumping your feet back to their starting position. Stand and reach your arms over your head. Jump quickly into the air so you land back where you started. As soon as you land with your knees bent, get into a squat position and do another repetition.

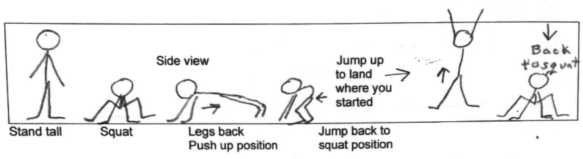

Stand tall   Squat   Legs back
Push up position   Jump back to squat position

Burpees Cont.

FULL-RANGE SQUATS

Stand with your feet hip-width apart with your arms by your side or out in front of you. Bend your knees and lower your body to the ground as if you are going to sit on a chair. Stop as your knees reach a 90-degree angle or farther. Hold the squat position for two seconds. Return to the starting position while squeezing your glutes.

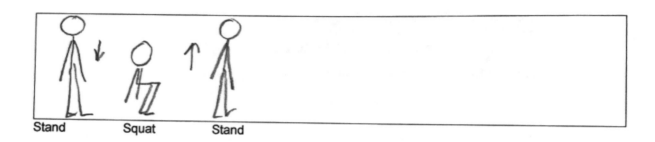

Stand   Squat   Stand

HUG LUNGES

Stand upright with feet about hip-width apart. Raise your right knee and grasp it with both hands while pointing your toes upward toward your shin. Next, raise up on the toes of your left foot. Let go of your knee and step forward into a lunge. Come up out of the lunge and raise the opposite leg to repeat on the opposite side. This completes one rep. Repeat as necessary.

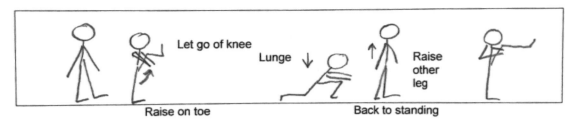

Let go of knee

Lunge ↓

Raise other leg

Raise on toe

Back to standing

Hug Lunges Cont.

STEP OVER HURDLES FORWARD AND BACKWARD

You are stepping over an imaginary hurdle. Forward step over hurdle starts by bringing the foot that isn't on the ground (lead leg) up to your butt and then quickly extend it up over the hurdle. Drag the trail leg sideways over the side of the hurdle after the lead leg has passed over. The ankle and the knee are supposed to be the same distance from the ground. Backward step over hurdles repeats the process the opposite way.

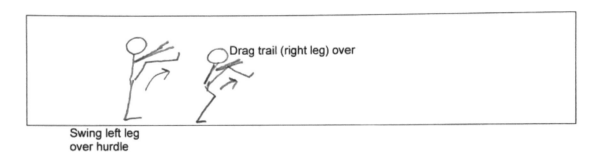

Drag trail (right leg) over

Swing left leg over hurdle

WARMUP AND STRETCHING (IF THERE'S NOT VERY MUCH ROOM TO MOVE AROUND)

Sometimes we find ourselves in a situation where you have to get ready to play a match but don't have a lot of room to move around. Try to find as big a place as possible to warm up, but a great tennis warmup can be achieved with a space as little as 3x5 feet square. Example: it doesn't require hardly any space to do some racket hops over the handle of your racket with both feet. You can even get a great warmup without using any equipment. Squats, progressive twisting lunges, split steps, volley shadow swings, etc., are examples of good tennis-specific movements that can be done in a small space. If you have the space to do full-range shadow swings like mentioned in the paragraphs above, by all means, don't pass that up.

Another effective way to warm up when there is very little space available is dynamic stretching in a Tabata-style format, where you do an exercise for a determined number of seconds followed by some seconds of rest. A Tabata-style routine focuses on exerting a high exercise effort for a minimal amount of time, followed by a short rest. A Tabata workout consists of strength and aerobic exercises that work the entire body instead of just one or two particular sets of muscles.

Example #1

Thirty seconds of squats, 10 seconds rest, 30 seconds of mountain climbers, 10 seconds rest, etc. You can also vary the lengths of your seconds if your time to play is sooner than later. Example: 20 seconds of squats, 5 seconds rest, 20 seconds of mountain climbers, 5 seconds rest. You can use your phone to time yourself, have someone time you, or just do a count in your head. Or you can do a number of determined exercises and dynamic stretches before moving on to the next activity. Example: 15 pushups, 15 burpees, 15 alternating lunges, 15 jumping jacks, 15 arm circles, 15 leg swings on both sides, etc. You can also do more than one set if time permits. A Tabata-style warmup is a good way to mimic the action of a tennis match where you have a flurry of activity for mostly a short while, followed by short breaks before the next point begins.

EXERCISE DESCRIPTIONS: Alternating Lunges, Arm Circles, Mountain Climbers, Burpees, Jumping Jacks, Squats

ALTERNATING LUNGES

Stand with feet shoulder-width apart, core engaged. To sink into a lunge, step back with your right foot and bend both knees until your left thigh is parallel to the floor. Return to starting position by gently pushing off your right foot, engaging your left glutes, and stepping forward. Repeat on the other side for alternating lunges.

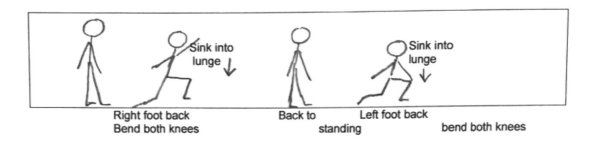

ARM CIRCLES

Stand up and extend your arms straight out by your sides. Your arms should be positioned parallel to the floor and perpendicular (at a 90-degree angle) to your torso. Place your feet shoulder-width apart. This will be your starting position. Slowly start to make small circles of about a foot in diameter with each of your outstretched arms at about shoulder height. With your arms forward, breathe normally as you perform the range of motion. Continue the circular motion with your outstretched arms for about ten seconds. Finally, reverse the movement as you continue the full exercise in the opposite direction.

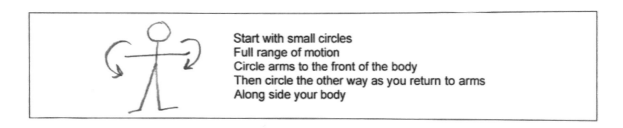

LEG SWINGS

Can be done using a chair or other object for balance or try to balance on your own. Start standing straight with your hands on your hips or to your sides. Swing one leg across the body and, using momentum, swing out to the side away from the body a determined number of times and repeat on the other side.

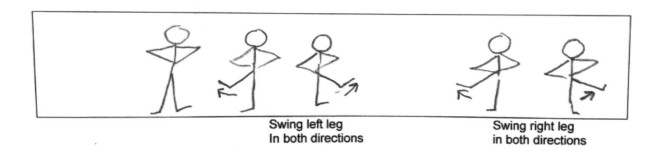

Swing left leg
In both directions

Swing right leg
in both directions

MOUNTAIN CLIMBERS

Start in a press-up position with your hands shoulder-width apart directly beneath your shoulders. As quickly as you can, pull your right knee towards your chest without letting it touch the floor, then return to the start position. Repeat step two with your left leg.

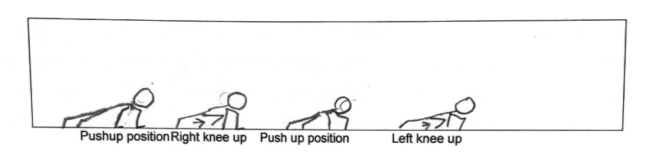

Pushup position Right knee up   Push up position   Left knee up

BURPEES

Standing tall, you start the exercise by going into a squat position with your knees bent, back straight, and your feet about shoulder-width apart. Lower the palms of your hands to the floor in front of you so they're just inside your feet. With your weight on your hands, kick your feet back so you're on your hands and toes in a pushup position. Keeping your body straight from head to heels, remember not to let your back sag or to stick your butt in the air. Do a frog kick by jumping your feet back to their starting position. Stand and reach your arms over your head. Jump quickly into the air and land back where you started. As soon as you land with your knees bent, get into a squat position and repeat.

| Stand | Squat | Push up position | Jump back bo squat | Jump up to stand |

JUMPING JACKS

Stand upright with your legs together and arms at your sides. Bend your knees slightly and jump into the air. As you jump, spread your legs until they are about shoulder-width apart. Stretch your arms out and over your head. Jump back to the starting position. Repeat.

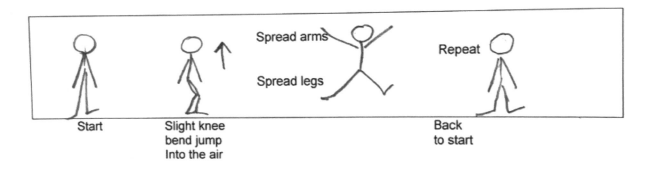

Spread arms
Spread legs
Repeat

Start — Slight knee bend jump Into the air — Back to start

SQUATS

Stand with your feet hip-width apart with your arms by your side or out in front of you. Bend your knees and lower your body to the ground as if you are going to sit on a chair. Stop when your knees reach a 90-degree angle or farther. Hold the squat position for two seconds. Return to the starting position while squeezing your glutes.

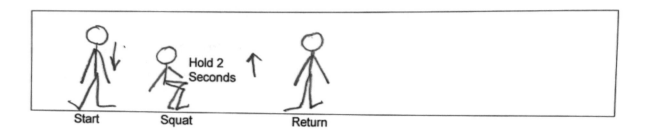

WARMUP AND STRETCHING (IF YOU HAVE PLENTY OF TIME AND ROOM BEFORE HAVING TO PLAY)

Every warmup starts with hydration; take a big drink from your water bottle, which should be as standard equipment as your tennis racket, and get started.

The ideal warmup would include doing everything for your warmup and dynamic stretching on a tennis court if one is available. If a court is not available, find space available where you can go back and forth or in a circle, like on a short track. You can also do a Tabata-style warmup where you use more space when you have the area to move around.

Do two to four minutes of light jogging, side shuffles, and skipping or other movements. Here is an example of a good tennis warmup after your minutes of dynamic stretching.

Put two tennis balls or similar objects about eight feet apart and do what I call a 5 to 30s. This is an individual warmup where a player increases by five reps each time they complete an exercise. For example: again, place two tennis balls about eight feet apart and lay your racket about two feet next to one of the balls. Start with five side shuffles without crossing your feet in a figure-8 pattern around the balls. Next, ten pushups, 15 racket hops with both feet together jumping over the racket handle, 20 full-range squats, 25 jumping jacks, and 30 mountain climbers. You can do more than one set if you'd like, even changing the exercises to emphasize different muscle groups. Below is an easier-to-read example of the 5 to 30s.

- 5 figure-8s around tennis balls
- 10 full-range pushups
- 15 full-range stationary squats
- 20 racket hops
- 25 jumping jacks
- 30 mountain climbers

Variation: Just do 5 to 15s, or 5 to 20s, or mix and match your favorite exercises.

Don't forget your full-range shadow swings of forehands, backhands, serves, and volleys. You can even throw in a series of split steps while moving side to side and forward.

EXERCISE DESCRIPTIONS: Squats, Mountain Climbers, Jumping Jacks, Cross Jacks, Side Shuffles

SQUATS

Stand with your feet hip-width apart with your arms by your side or out in front of you. Bend your knees and lower your body to the ground as if you are going to sit on a chair. Stop as your knees reach a 90-degree angle or farther. Hold the squat position for two seconds. Return to the starting position while squeezing your glutes.

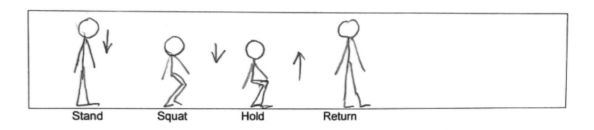

Stand   Squat   Hold   Return

Mountain Climbers

Start in a press-up position with your hands shoulder-width apart directly beneath your shoulders. As quickly as you can, pull your right knee towards your chest without letting it touch the floor, then return to the start position. Repeat step 2 with your left leg.

Push up position   Right knee up   Push up position   Left knee up
(as legs come up, no touching the ground)

JUMPING JACKS

Stand upright with your legs together and arms at your sides. Bend your knees slightly and jump into the air. As you jump, spread your legs to be about shoulder-width apart. Stretch your arms out and over your head. Jump back to starting position. Repeat.

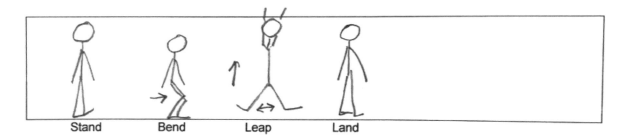

CROSS JACKS

Same as a jumping jack, except you cross your legs and arms as you jump. Left arm and left leg cross in front, then right arm and right leg cross in front. Continue alternating as you jump. The crossjack increased the range of motion.

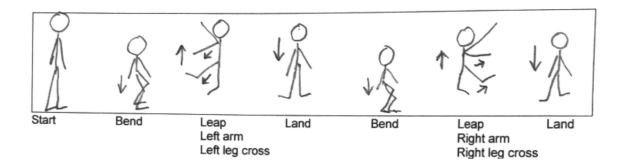

SIDE SHUFFLES

Same as the side slides except in the 5 to 30s example, it's done in a figure-8 pattern around two tennis balls eight feet apart.

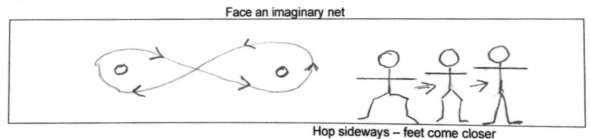

Face an imaginary net

Hop sideways – feet come closer together as you move along

Warmup – Hitting with a Partner

1. Warm Up

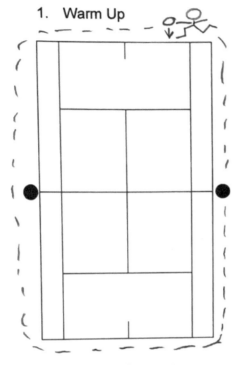

Bounce the ball while jogging slowly around the court, stopping every 5 yards to do a stretching exercise. For example:

Thigh Stretch

Calf Stretch

Hamstring Stretch
(leg on a bench)

Tricep Stretch

2. Hitting with a partner

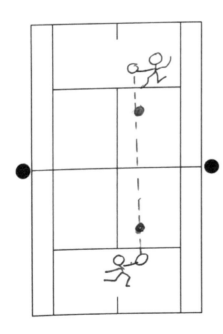

Standing a step behind the service line, passively block (little hit) cooperatively to a partner or coach (landing the ball inside the service box)

To add a little interest and help ensure cooperative hitting, place a target ball on court for players to aim for.

Encourage players to accentuate little hustle steps when waiting to receive a partner's hit.

3. Add a little more movement and add a racquet control drill

②Hit the ball over
to the other side
(let the ball bounce)

Or vice versa
Whichever side the
ball comes, hit it to
the other side

①. Receive the ball on this side
(backhand hit)

③.To hit the ball to partner
with a forehand hit

4. Both players hitting cooperatively (one player hits down the line, the partner hits cross court, then change

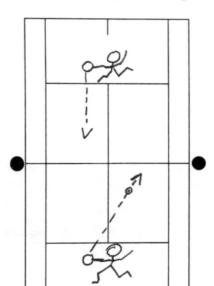

Hitting controlled shots in the service box, moving
the partner a few steps (friendly and cooperatively)

5. Cooperative rallying down the middle to each other

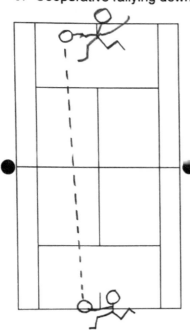

Counting consecutive hits to a certain number
(hitting with a rally speed) a little short of a winner

Add
1.   Cooperative rallying singles count deuce to deuce side
2.   Cooperative rallying singles court ad side to ad side

Counting consecutive hits to a certain number

6. Cooperative hitting volley to volley

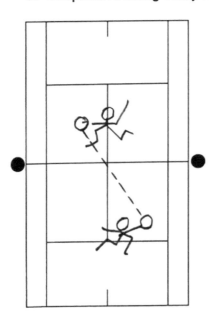

Counting hits
(try to volley, but, if necessary) hit a half volley

No passive baby volleys

No blasting winning volleys

Mix up forehands/backhands

7. Overheads

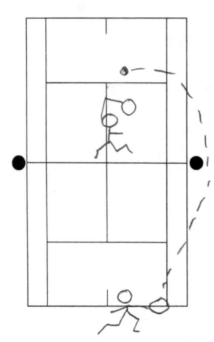

a. Player lobs up a high, comfortable ball
b. Player hits a medium speed overhead to the deuce side
c. Players rally out the overhead friendly
d. Player then hits the overhead to the ad side
e. Players rally out the overhead friendly.

Change ends after a few minutes.

8. Both players can warm up their serves before match conditions point play, Serving both 1st and 2nd serves to both sides.

If, for some reason, there is a lengthy pause during the on court warm up, keep moving with moderate intensity to simulate stroking the various shots to stay warm, loose and focused.

AN INDIVIDUAL MOVEMENT AND PHYSICAL FITNESS WORKOUT

The type of fitness workout required to help prepare a tennis player for competition is very specific and closely related to the physical requirements of match play. Most matches are a long, drawn-out, physically exhausting affair.

What type of physical movements is a tennis player required to do? Tennis players are not required to run two to three consecutive miles in the game situation. Running long distances would certainly help build up a player's general cardiovascular efficiency, but a specific workout, including running dozens of short, three- to five-yard sprints with a racquet in hand, simulating the strokes and movements a tennis player performs in a match situation, would be more relevant.

Players exercising under this pressure, with perspiration dripping into their eyes, and neuromuscular tremors in their legs, and still expected to perform well, will experience this in the closing moments of a big match.

It would be valuable to occasionally include a long two to three miles run, followed immediately by point play against an opponent. The players would be simulating the feeling and effort required to compete in the closing stages of a tough, long match.

What types of movements is a player forced to make when playing a match?

On the next page is a diagram of the five movements that a player makes when playing a match.

#1 Hitting groundstrokes along the baseline

#2 Moving up to the net chasing a short ball or hitting an approach shot

#5 Chasing a ball down that has been lobbed over their head

#4 Skipping back to hit an overhead

#3 Moving across the net to volley/overhead a short lob

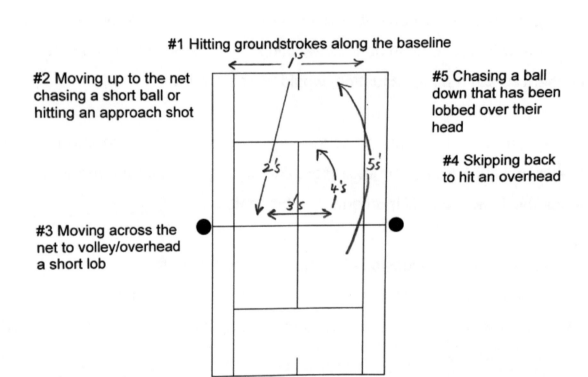

Which movements, in order of frequency, is a player most likely to have to perform?

Regardless of players or style of play, the following is usually true:

In order of frequency, the movements most often used are:

    1s – moving along the baseline

    2s – coming to the net, making an approach shot, or chasing a short ball

    3s – volleying at the net

    4s – from the net, moving back for an overhead

    5s – running down an overhead lob

Which combination of movements occurs most often?

    1s to 2s

    3s to 4s

    1s to 2s to 3s to 4s to 5s

Some combinations are impossible. For example, 1s followed by 3s.

It would be realistic to combine the numbers that naturally follow each other in the game situation. For example

- Practicing a 1 – 2 – 4 sequence of movement.
- 1 - moving along the baseline
- 2 – moving to the net or a short ball approach shot
- 4 – skipping back to hit an overhead winner

On Court Movement and Physical Fitness

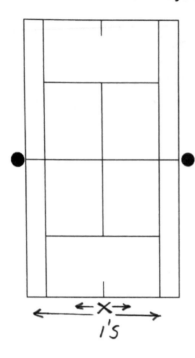

1's

A player calls out the movements under his/her breath.

1's moving along the baseline

Start at the X.

Call out under your breath, then move to simulate with good technique.

A mixture of sequences returning to the start after simulating the stroke.

Short Forehand	Short Backhand
Wide Backhand	Short Backhand

(working on footwork/strokes/fitness)

To begin, go for 1 minute.

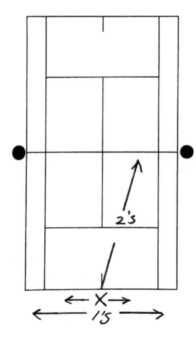

2's
1's

1's and 2's Baseline, coming to net

Start at the X.

Call out a variety of 1's for about 15 seconds, then call out "short forehand drop shot" or "short backhand drop shot".

Then hustle up to simulate hitting a drop shot or pushing the ball up the line.

Then recover to repeat.

To begin, do 3 repetitions.

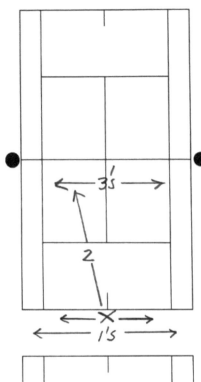

1's and 2's and 3's

Start at the X.

Call out under your breath a couple of 1's, then a 2, then a couple of 3's.

Short Forehand   Wide Forehand
Short Backhand Drop Shot
Backhand Volley   Forehand volley

Remember to return to the middle after simulating the stroke.

Then recover to the start position X.

To begin, do 3 repetitions.

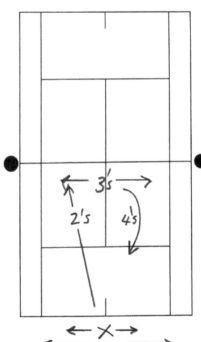

1's, 2's, 3's, 4's

Start at the X.

Call out a couple of 1's (short or wide).

Then call out a 2 (short backhand drop shot).

Next, call out 3 3's (backhand volley, backhand volley, forehand volley).

Then call out a 4 (overhead smash).

Then recover to the start position of X.

To begin, do 3 repetitions.

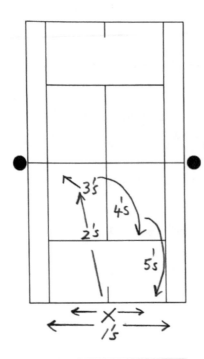

1's, 2's, 3's, 4's, 5's

Start at the X.

Call out a couple of 1's (short or wide).

Then call out a 2 (short backhand drop shot) and a 3 (backhand volley).

Then call out a 4 (overhead smash), then call out another 3 (forehand volley), then call out a 5 (chase the ball down to the deuce corner and lob).

Then recover to the start position.

To begin, do 3 repetitions.

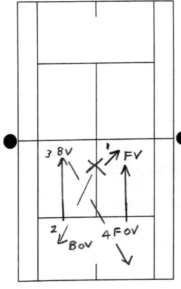

Make up the number sequence you need to work on.

For example, you might need to work on 3's and 4's.

Start at the X.

Follow the numbers and simulate a technically sound stroke.

1 Start out by moving up to hit a forehand volley.
2 Hustle back to hit a backhand overhead.
3 Move forward to hit a backhand volley.
4 Hustle back to hit a regular overhead.
1   Move forward to hit a forehand volley.

Start the sequence again.

WHAT SPECIFIC COMPONENTS OF PHYSICAL FITNESS NEED DEVELOPING FOR YOU TO BECOME A BETTER TENNIS PLAYER?

Agility

Agility is the ability to change direction or body position quickly.

Mobility

Mobility is the ability to move a joint through its full range of movement.

Speed

Speed is a player's ability to move quickly.

Muscular Endurance

Muscular endurance is the ability to maintain a movement at submaximal muscular effort.

Muscular Strength

It would be important to recognize the muscles that contribute most to the execution of the various tennis strokes.

Once the stroke movements and muscular analysis has been made, beneficial exercises could be recommended. A muscleman will not necessarily be a good tennis player. Timing, coordination, shot selection, anticipation, and improvisation all help to mold a successful tennis player. However, a certain level of strength and endurance is necessary, especially in the specific tennis muscles.

SETTING UP YOUR PERSONAL PHYSICAL FITNESS PROGRAM

I strongly recommend a consultation with a qualified physical fitness professional or trainer to work with you and your tennis coach to customize a program to cover your specific physical fitness needs.

For example:

   a) Strengthen specific muscle areas.

   b) Work on flexibility to help your range of motion.

   c) Improve cardiovascular endurance.

   d) Improve agility, mobility, increase speed over a short distance.

   e) Improve reflexes.

   f) Groove stroke techniques.

   g) Work on improving anticipation and decision-making.

Note: There is a definite link between physical fitness development and the development of a player's strokes and strategies. So, the team working with the tennis coach and the physical fitness professional is extremely important.

PUFF! PUFF! TAKE OUT THE GARBAGE? NOW?

Chapter 9

Tennis Stories

LIST OF STORIES

- A Clinic I Would Like to Do Over
- Chance Meeting with John McEnroe
- An Opportunity to Hang Out with Rod Laver
- Teaming Up with Allen Fox To Play a Set That Really Counted
- Tennis Can Be Played From the Cradle to the Grave
- Some Attributes Transcend Sports
- Handling Adversity on a Train Ride
- An Amazing Shot I Made as a 16-year-old and Haven't Duplicated Since
- Let Your Emotions Come Out – If You Are an Emotional Player – But Do It the Right Way
- Are You Unable to Get into the Match? Keep Trying. Momentum Swings Do Happen.
- Three Encounters with the Animal World
  - ◊ Teaching Betsy Miller
  - ◊ Tournament play in the Australian Countryside
  - ◊ Featured Speaker at the Fourth International Symposium of the Spanish Tennis Federation
- Representing the USTA in Saudi Arabia
- Handling Adversity on a Plane Flight
- A Short Story from a Trip to Singapore

- My Most Memorable Set of Tennis
- Most Unusual Presentation
- Introducing Players with Their Winning Records
- An Exercise in Making Adjustments and Staying Under Control
- Who Are You Playing For?
- Mike and Bob Bryan's Wonderful Gesture
- A Tennis Program that Included the Whole Family
- My Most Heartwarming and Emotional Tennis Coaches Workshop
- 2021 USTA Tennis Teacher's Conference Faculty Emeritus Award

A CLINIC I WOULD LIKE TO DO OVER

It was my first year of teaching at a tennis club.

As a young tennis coach, I worked a full day teaching lessons. I taught three hours of ladies' group lessons in the morning, took a trip home for a quick lunch, and returned in the afternoon for five hours of private and junior group lessons.

So much of my work was new and exciting, and being young and energetic, it didn't seem like a difficult workload. Occasionally, I got a little nervous, but loved my job and wanted to do well.

A new session of ladies' group lessons started on a Monday morning: three one-hour groups with eight ladies on two courts for a total of 24 ladies who were excited to hit tennis balls, learn some skills, and have a good time. On the morning of the first day of lessons, I woke up early and really hustled to shower, shave, and eat a healthy breakfast, wanting to get to the club early to set up the teaching stations.

In my rush to get out the door and to the club on time, I cut myself while shaving, treated the slight bleeding cut on my neck, and still made it on time!

Ball baskets out, water containers filled on each court, and nets measured to the right height, I was ready to go! In short, the lessons went well; 24 happy ladies. Then lunchtime came. I had an hour off for lunch, so I drove the five minutes home to enjoy lunch with my wife, Janet. I skipped up the stairs to our apartment and enthusiastically gave Janet a hug and told her the ladies classes went well. Janet said nothing. She just stared at me, looking shocked.

"What?" I said.

She very slowly and softly whispered, "How long has that small piece of toilet paper been hanging from your neck?"

"Oh, my gosh! Are you kidding me?!" I exclaimed.

I knew immediately what had happened. In my haste to get to the club, I had grabbed a small piece of toilet paper to render first aid to my shaving cut and had forgotten to take it off. Three hours of teaching and all accomplished with a piece of toilet paper hanging from my neck! I was one embarrassed tennis coach! The ladies were too nice to mention it, but I learned my lesson to slow down—make sure. I never make the same mistake twice!

CHANCE MEETING WITH JOHN MCENROE

In the mid-1970s, I was the Director of Tennis at the West Hills Racquet Club in Portland, Oregon.

One of our club members was Nike co-founder and CEO Philip Knight. Phil called me one morning and asked if I was free early afternoon for a social game of doubles. He said, "I have this young kid from New York flying in for a few days, and I intend to sign him with a Nike contract."

"Sure, I'm happy to do that," I said.

We met the young kid and his father. The kid introduced himself as John McEnroe. Phil Knight and I played a set against John and his dad. They won the set 7-5. I remember saying to Phil, "This kid has amazing racquet control!" The set we played was a social set where we took turns hitting winners. John demonstrated his racquet control a couple of times by slicing a short ball over to our court with the ball bouncing on our side of the net and then returning to John's side without us being able to hit the ball. *Are you kidding me?* I thought. I would have needed a frame shot, a high wind advantage, and a lot of luck to pull off a shot like that.

When sitting around enjoying a social drink and chatting after the set, Phil smiled and jokingly asked John, "Of course, you're going to win Wimbledon this year—right?" We all chuckled a little.

John didn't win that year, but he did win three Wimbledon men's singles titles and a total of seven Grand Slam singles titles during his career. Today, the Nike Tennis building on the Nike Campus in Beaverton, Oregon, is called The John McEnroe Building.

I consider John one of the all-time greats.

AN OPPORTUNITY TO HANG OUT WITH ROD LAVER

In the early 1980s, I was in Los Angeles to give a presentation at the annual USPTA Southern California Tennis Coaches Conference. I was excited to see that tennis great Rod Laver was also presenting a session. He was scheduled to speak on the court after me, so I stayed behind after my session to try and meet him.

I approached him and said, "Hi, Rod. I am an Aussie, too. It's an honor to meet you. What are you going to talk on?"

He replied, "I don't know. I don't really do these sorts of events."

I said, "The coaches present already have their own philosophy of techniques and strategies. They probably would like to hear your stories about winning two Grand Slams, one as an amateur and one as a professional. Then let them hit a few balls with you." I continued, "Let me help you. I could stay in the background and orchestrate to set up the session."

I knew then he could glow like the star he was.

I organized two lines of coaches, and the first in each line would come forward to rally with Rod. I had Rod at the net, knowing it would be more comfortable for him to block back volleys rather than hustle at the baseline, hitting groundstrokes. I stood next to Rod at the net with a ball basket, feeding balls for him to hit as needed.

We went through about 80 coaches in 30 minutes. The coaches were excited to hit with Rod Laver.

After rallying, I initiated a question-and-answer session. I started by asking Rod, "Of the two Grand Slams you've won, which was the most difficult to win—the Amateurs Only or the Professionals?"

"You think it would have been the Open slams, but according to the players I've had to beat, the Amateurs was the toughest," he said.

The attending coaches followed with some great questions and were spellbound by Rod's candid responses and good humor. The session went on for another 20 minutes with only one quiet lull, where I filled in and asked Rod a question. "What is your best tip on mental toughness?"

"You shouldn't have to beat two players to win a singles match," he replied.

That answer was golden but needed a little thought. What Rod meant was: a player shouldn't have to work to control his own negative, destructive emotions before trying to beat an opponent.

It was a worthwhile session. Everyone felt good. And everyone won. The session was filed away under the successful column!

TEAMING UP WITH ALLEN FOX TO PLAY A SET THAT REALLY COUNTED

In the mid-1980s, the International Tennis Federation (ITF) invited Allen Fox and me to represent them at a Spanish coaches symposium in Granada, Spain. Quite a large number (300-400) of coaches attended the three-day symposium. I spoke on a variety of topics, and Allen spoke on his specialty of mental games.

Allen was an outstanding player, ranked as high as #4 in US Men's Singles, and was in the top ten in the United States five times between 1961-68. He was a quarter-finalist at Wimbledon in 1965. Allen was a great player. I was not a great player but a good one, having played Division 1 tennis for seven years in both Australia and the United States, at the University of Melbourne, Western Australia University, and the University of Oregon.

We teamed up to play the set of our lives. Toward the end of the second day of the Granada Symposium, the Spanish coaches that organized the symposium asked if Allen and I could play a set against two of the attending coaches. Allen and I looked at each other, and probably both felt like we were really going to be tested. Were we being set up to play against two of the best players attending the symposium? Probably so!

As we warmed up, ready to play the set in front of the several hundred attendees, I remember saying to Allen, "If we lose this set, you know that *no one* will show up tomorrow to listen to our presentations."

Allen played the deuce side, and his strength—pinpoint groundstrokes—was on. I played the ad side, and my strength—net play—was on. We won the set 6-4. Phew!

All was well with the world!

TENNIS CAN BE PLAYED FROM THE CRADLE TO THE GRAVE

The World Masters Games were held in Portland, Oregon, in August 1998. It's a quadrennial event that attracts thousands of master athletes from over 100 countries for the world's largest participatory multi-sport competition, including tennis.

My doubles partner and I won four matches to win the Men's 50s Doubles title.

The week-long competition included a number of social events that helped round out a truly wonderful week. One event was very memorable. It was an exhibition doubles match that involved two area college players, a seven-year-old advanced beginning boy, and the oldest competitor in the 85 and over men's draw—a 103-year-old player from England. Teams warmed up; they looked fairly even. One college player with the young seven-year-old and the other college player with the English centenarian.

I remember having heartwarming thoughts of how wonderful the game of tennis was. Here was a match where the players' ages ranged from seven to 103. They were getting great exercise, having fun, and entertaining the crowd.

The two college players kept the ball going and were good enough to make sure that everyone had an opportunity to hit a winning shot. They were like "enzymes" that kept the rallies going.

The match was very even. The crowd enthusiastically clapped and cheered the rallies. They really enjoyed the exhibition.

The event was filed under the successful column. Who won? Everyone—the players, the crowd, and the game of tennis.

SOME ATTRIBUTES TRANSCEND SPORTS

My partner and I were playing in the Oregon State Seniors 50 and Over State Doubles final against two players that played well. One opponent was tall and a big server with good volleys, and his partner was very consistent.

As the match progressed, I noted that the tall opponent's mental game was way ahead of his strokes and strategies. My partner tried to rattle him with verbal comments like "So lucky!" (just loud enough to be heard) when he lost a volley exchange with the tall one. The tall opponent showed no reaction when missing an easy ball. My partner's attempt to verbally intimidate him was not working. Who was this guy? We managed to win the match in three close sets.

Following the match, I sat courtside with the tall one and began chatting with him. "Where did you play college tennis?" I asked.

"I didn't play college tennis," he said. "I took up tennis about ten years ago and really enjoyed playing. I play almost every day. I was a baseball pitcher in college and played as a professional in New York for ten years."

Are you kidding me!? No wonder my partner's verbal jabs had no effect on shaking up the tall one's concentration. He had seen and heard it all as a world-class pitcher. I couldn't wait to tell my partner the tall one's true identity!

HANDLING ADVERSITY ON A TRAIN RIDE

One of my favorite events I've held annually since 1975 is a one-day, five-session tennis workshop for high school, club, and college tennis coaches (also parents of junior tennis players). Signups vary anywhere between 30 and 100 participants.

Sometime in the late 70s, Joan Armstrong, a high school coach from Mt. Vernon, Washington, drove the five hours to Portland to attend the workshop. I was honored to learn she traveled so far to participate in my workshop. She was very enthusiastic about the workshop and asked if I was interested and available to travel to her hometown of Mt. Vernon to present a day of tennis-related topics to the Washington state area coaches. "Love to. I would enjoy doing that," I said.

We set a suitable date, a Saturday two months ahead. I would travel up to Mt. Vernon after my Friday workday and present my program all day Saturday. I thought about my travel arrangements and decided that a five- to six-hour car drive was a little tough following a teaching day, so I decided to travel by train through Seattle to Mt. Vernon late that Friday afternoon. I would arrive in Mt. Vernon a shade before 9 pm. It was doable.

The trip day arrived. I had packed a fresh set of tennis clothes, my notes, and handouts. I was ready to go. My Friday teaching was comfortable, but I was ready for a restful trip and remember thinking it was a good decision to travel by train rather than by car for the five-hour trip north on I-5. I ordered a light meal and a warm drink and got myself cozy for the long trip. The rhythmic clacking of the train moving along the tracks lulled me to sleep. I was out like a light.

I must have been more tired than I thought because I slept longer than I'd intended. I woke with a start to the announcement: "Bellingham station next stop." *Are you kidding me?* I thought. I must have slept right through the Mt. Vernon stop. Bellingham was way north of Mt. Vernon, and the next stop after Bellingham was in Canada!

Keep calm, I told myself. Just pretend that Bellingham was my stop and get off the train. I pictured the train stopping at Mt. Vernon and Joan Armstrong straining her eyes to see me get off the train, but no Til!

The Bellingham train station at 10 pm was a semi-dark and desolate place. Everything was closed, including the ticket office, and no one was walking around. There was nothing, nobody, just two dim lights on the station platform. I wasn't totally scared, but I was close!

The eerie atmosphere prompted me to take a tennis racquet out of my bag and have it on hand if I had to protect myself from someone or something. My heart was racing.

I was calm enough to recognize that I had to call Joan Armstrong in Mt. Vernon. I noticed a phone booth and had some change in my pocket. This was before cell phones.

Joan was very understanding. "I will drive up to the Bellingham train station to pick you up," she said. "The drive is about 45 minutes."

I remember pacing up and down the semi-dark train station to stay warm and nervously reacting to the occasional sounds of station machinery and animal noises.

Joan arrived, and we headed south on I-5 to her home in Mt. Vernon. I apologized and thanked her profusely. She remained understanding and just replied, "Things happen. No worries."

By the time we arrived at Joan's home, it was past midnight. "What time is the first session scheduled for?" I asked.

"8 am," she replied. "We have to sleep fast."

The morning came quickly. I was pumped up and excited to meet the workshop attendees and start the program. My sleep deprivation was totally offset by my enthusiasm to do a good job in the presentations.

Joan did a great job setting up the teaching facility in her school's gym—a tennis net strung across the gym floor, a large rolling basket of new tennis balls, lots of seating close by, and a large open area and extensive wall space for activities.

At the end of the day, the attendees were happy, Joan was happy, and I was happy, too.

All's well that ends well. Way to fight, Gundars!

AN AMAZING SHOT I MADE AS A 16-YEAR-OLD AND HAVEN'T DUPLICATED SINCE

As a tennis player, I have always played brave, standing my ground when my opponent had an easy put away shot and always trying to return the ball.

There was one exceptional case where I turned my back on my opponent and made myself into a small ball so that I wouldn't get hit.

It was 1960, and I was playing in a boys' 17 and under match at a club tournament in Maryborough, just outside Melbourne in Australia. Michael, my opponent, was positioned a few feet from the net when he hit a drop shot that just cleared the net. I anticipated that shot and hustled up to the net to return it. I made it just in time but was not able to hit an effective shot; just lucky enough to pop the ball up into the air to give Michael an easy sitter shot. I was three feet from his racquet. My life was in danger. That's when I made myself into a small ball and turned my back to him.

Michael recognized that I had given up on trying to return his shot, casually blocking the ball over the net. Even though I was in a fetal position and was facing the other way, I left my racquet up in the air with the butt of my racquet pointed at Michael.

The improbable happened. Michael's block volley hit the butt of my racquet and returned to his side of the court for a winner. "Did my shot hit your hand?" he gasped.

"No," I replied. "It rebounded off the butt of my racquet." "You're kidding!" he yelled. "I think you won the point."

And I had a once-in-a-lifetime butt shot, never to be repeated!

LET YOUR EMOTIONS COME OUT – IF YOU ARE AN EMOTIONAL PLAYER – BUT DO IT THE RIGHT WAY!

Most coaches would agree that a certain amount of competitive emotion is a good thing.

The last thing we want to see is an emotionless and passive player struggling to get involved in a match. Getting fired up and putting on a game face are important parts of competing. There is nothing wrong with letting spectators know that you are in it, that you have good intensity and have come to play. However, the quality of a player's emotions must be kept in check—quality control.

This is a true story.

In the winter of 1994, I had just finished an on-court session at a tennis coaches convention in Chicago, Illinois. One of the attendees stayed behind to ask a question. "Til," he said, "I have a problem that I want to run by you and get your advice on."

"Fine," I said. "I have time."

The coach began his story. He was teaching a young boy who was a jerk. He yelled profanity after unforced errors and even threw and kicked his racquet when his serve was broken. He was a walking nightmare. The coach didn't want to suspend or disqualify the boy from tennis in any way because his mother, who was nice, also took lessons from him, and between the two of them, put a $400 check on his dinner table every month. He didn't want to upset them.

"What can I do with the kid?" he asked.

My response to the situation, and others like it is, "Let the kid yell and throw his racquet."

The coach stood, as many others do, stunned with an open-mouthed expression. "Are you sure?" he asked.

"Absolutely," I said. "Your player is obviously a highly energetic, emotional person, so let him express and vent his feelings. To expect him to take on the role of a passive jellyfish would just not be his style. Instead, teach him *how* to yell and throw his racquet."

Yelling bad words is negative, not good, and wrong. A coach should teach players like this to yell (only occasionally) phrases that are either motivational or instructional. "Come on, let's go!" is okay. "Don't rush the shot, take your time, pick a target" is okay. Slapping the thigh is okay. Tell the player they can occasionally yell but only the right stuff—nothing rude, degrading, disrespectful, or obnoxious. Teach them to throw their racquets. Throwing a racquet down toward the court is not acceptable. They will soon have tournament directors, umpires, and coaches reprimanding them. Throwing your racquet up in the air or batting it up into the air with an open palm (ironically, the same distance the racquet would go down to the court) and catching it is okay.

Spectators will say, "Isn't that cute?!" If you tell players to use the right words and throw their racquets in the right direction (and catch them!), they *can* play energized, intense matches and survive with good court etiquette. Doing this will stop their emotions from getting the best of them.

If players express their emotions in the manner described above, it might even help them.

ARE YOU UNABLE TO GET INTO THE MATCH? KEEP TRYING. MO-MENTUM SWINGS *DO* HAPPEN

I remember watching a girls' junior singles match in the 1997 Australian Open. One of the players was the master, hitting solid shots, moving the opponent around the court, and finishing points. In short, she was in charge. Her opponent was struggling just to stay upright and finish the match. She looked tentative, nervous, and was on the outside looking in. The score reflected my observation (6-0, 3-0 for the master).

I wandered the courts watching other matches but periodically came back to check on this particular match. On one of my return trips, I was amazed to find the master up only 4-3 in the second set. Her opponent was coming back; she had found a way to crawl into the match and was competing. I was excited for her and stayed to watch. The rallies were longer now; the points went back and forth; they both played some great tennis. To shorten the story, the master won the match 6-0, 6-4, hanging on for dear life as her opponent really came after her.

I approached the heroic come-back girl, shook her hand, and said, "Congratulations, good job."

She looked at me with an expression that said, *You crazy man, why are you congratulating me? I'm the loser.*

I felt I had to explain myself. "You had a tough time getting into the match," I said. "It's a credit to you to find a way to get into the match and compete. You can be proud of your effort." After a few more minutes of conversation, she finally realized why I so enthusiastically congratulated her.

She said, "Thank you." She felt better, and I felt happy to have seen the match. All was well with the world.

I have spent considerable time over the past few years asking tennis sports psychologists the following question: what can I tell my players to do when they are having a tough time getting into a match? In short, what should I do when my players aren't playing like they do in practice?

I was looking for practical, hands-on information that my players could use on tho court. Sometimes, my psychologist friends would give me advice that was too academic, too "airy fairy," and not really usable during match play. So, I would ask them the same question the next day. "You asked me that question yesterday!" they would say.

"Yes, I did," I would say. "And unless you can give me a good answer, I'm going to ask you the same question again tomorrow."

After asking this question repeatedly, here are some ideas I have gathered on what coaches should tell players who struggle to get into matches. Here are seven suggestions to help players get into a match:

1. Arrive at the match venue early to familiarize yourself with the match area and playing conditions. Mentally review your game plan, keeping it simple: keep the ball going, wait for your opponent to make a mistake, or for you to get an opportunity to finish the point.

2. Hit safe, solid shots down the middle of the court until your confidence and rhythm feel good.

3. Get into the point by serving a fast second serve for your first serve. When receiving, return your opponent's serve deep down the middle of the court.

4. Verbalize cue words under your breath, such as "early," just prior to ball contact point. This will help you focus on the present and force you to watch the ball more closely.

5. Between points, take the 20 seconds to walk along the baseline, breathing deeply and rhythmically and reviewing your game plan.

6. A tightly strung, nervous player is often stiff and immobile, almost robotic. So, do the reverse: talk a little more and move a lot to loosen up, particularly in the warmup.

7. Players can give themselves a little extra time to settle into a match, letting their opponent serve first.

THREE ENCOUNTERS WITH THE ANIMAL WORLD

Teaching Betsy Miller

This incident occurred at the West Hills Racquet Club in Portland, Oregon, in the mid-70s.

On a fairly warm, clear, blue-sky day, Betsy and I were having a lesson on outdoor court #3. It was a beautiful fall day!

I was helping Betsy with her service toss, and we spent a lot of time "lifting" the ball up into the air and looking up at the sky. We stopped our lesson when we noticed a beautiful scene—up high in the sky, thousands of geese flying over the top of us, heading south to California for the winter. It was an awesome sight we were delighted to experience. A few minutes later, after the flock (actually, a group of geese flying overhead is called a skein) had disappeared, we heard a "plop, plop" sound. Something had landed on our court. I remember thinking, *"It can't be raining; it's a sunny, blue-sky day*. It wasn't rain, of course; the birds were bombing us even though they were long gone.

Are you kidding me? No!

Tournament Play in the Australian Countryside

As a junior player in the early 1960s, playing in a small country tournament about three hours northwest of Melbourne, I was housed in a small trailer house a stone's throw from the tennis club. Each evening after returning to my trailer, I would leave my sweaty, odorous tennis shoes on the steps outside the trailer to dry out overnight. The next day, I would have a dry, well-rested pair of tennis shoes waiting for me.

After the first match on the final day of the tournament (which happened to be a tough three-set win), I removed my tennis shoes to rest my feet by putting on my sandals. When I was removing my tennis shoes, I looked down at my socks and noticed what I thought was a stick. I knocked this stick off my sock, and it landed on the ground. On closer inspection, this stick looked like it had hairs on it and showed signs of slight movement. Was this stick coming from inside my tennis shoe? I looked inside my shoe, and to my horror, there it was, a squashed spider in the toe of my shoe. What!?

I looked more closely at my sock, and it had gooey stuff on it. I threw my sock away! I played the whole match with a spider in my tennis shoe. Are you kidding me!? The spider must have crawled into my shoe while it was being aired out overnight on the trailer steps.

What did I learn from this dilemma? Check your shoes if they are left outside overnight. Also, if you want to win a match in three sets, put a spider in your shoe!

Featured Speaker at the Fourth International Symposium of the Spanish Tennis Federation

At the symposium's grand finale, there was an evening banquet and a professional bullfight at the neighborhood ring. I accepted the challenge of a bullfight.

Following the main display of bullfighting with real live, mature bulls, the bullfighters came out into the ring with a young bull. Some coaches at the symposium volunteered to go into the ring to playfully fight this young bull (the size of the biggest dog I have ever seen and a couple of inches of actual horns). As the night was concluding, the chant came out from the 300+ coach attendees for Til to take on the young bull. "Til, Til, Til," they chanted.

My two coaching friends who invited me to speak at the symposium smiled and nodded to go for it. Juan Carlos Andrade and Jose Antonio Arrantz started to coach me. Jose took off his red coat and gave it to me to use. And I know enough of watching bullfights in movies that the red cape had to be out to the side and not in front of you. I became El Matador Tilmanis!

I was a little scared. It was probably the biggest match of my life. The young bull came by me into Jose's jacket two to three times.

I think they wanted to make it a memorable trip. They succeeded!

REPRESENTING THE USTA IN SAUDI ARABIA

In February 1979, I traveled to Saudi Arabia to represent the USTA International Tennis Teaching Project and to serve as a consultant to the Saudi Tennis and Table Tennis Federation.

My mission was to offer the Federation a program of tennis development that included teacher training, the formation of a tournament system, an assessment of facilities and equipment needs, and the composition of an instructional workbook in Arabic.

For one week, I traveled to Jeddah, Dammam, and Riyadh, talking to tennis coaches and visiting tennis clubs and universities. I very conscientiously asked questions, closely observing, making insightful conclusions, and formulating some innovative ideas for the development of Saudi tennis. In short, I gathered much information to present to Saudi Tennis and Table Tennis Association President Almalik. My plan was to return to the United States, write up my report, and then send it back to the Association.

The day before returning to the United States, Mr. Almalik said, "Of course, you will be presenting your findings on developing the future of Saudi tennis to the council tomorrow."

I remember making a concerted effort to confidently say, "Yes, of course." Then noticed my mind balking and thinking, *Get the report together and present it in the morning.*

I put several comfortable pillows behind my back, sat at the hotel desk, and spent the rest of the night writing my report to present the next morning. In short, the presentation went well. My most memorable all-nighter of academic preparation—a feeling very similar to cramming for my college finals at the University of Oregon. I mailed a more detailed 12-page report after returning to the United States.

It was a very positive, memorable trip; I was treated royally. It was an eye-opening trip as well. I can remember giving a tennis demonstration at a college for Saudi princes and staying to enjoy lunch with them. I sat at a round table with six Saudi princes and noticed that all of us had a huge plate with a metal cover over it. When it looked like we were starting to each lunch, I removed the metal cover over my plate and, to my surprise, noted a whole chicken in the middle with a large portion of a variety of vegetables around it. I quickly thought, *Is the chicken for the whole table? I scanned the rest of the table*. Everyone uncovered their plates to reveal a whole chicken and accompaniments.

Are you kidding me!? No! It was a delicious, very filling, and memorable lunch!

HANDLING ADVERSITY ON A PLANE FLIGHT

On April 20, 1991, I flew out of Portland, Oregon, and headed to Buenos Aires, Argentina. My mission, representing the ITF, was to present a three-day Tennis Coaches Seminar for Argentinian tennis coaches.

I booked my flight with my regular travel agent, going from Portland to Miami to Buenos Aires and the return. When departing from Miami for the international flight, the travel agent asked if I had a visa to get into Argentina. I said that my travel agent told me I didn't need one. The Miami gate agent said I did because I held an Australian passport, and Argentina would not let me into the country without a visa. I told the agent I had a letter of invitation from an Argentinian government organization with me, and I thought I should be okay to get into the country. The gate agent replied that many travelers had been denied entry without a visa.

I knew the national tennis coach and Argentinian tennis officials were meeting me at the airport, so I assured the agent that I would be okay. After all, I had a letter of invitation in my travel bag. Was I taking a risk? I went ahead and boarded the flight to Buenos Aires.

As it turned out, I was, indeed, taking a risk! After landing in the Buenos Aires airport, I was told that I could not enter the country without a stamped visa in my passport. I chatted through the fence with my host, Gustavo Granitto, the Argentinian national coach. He told me that the top official at the airport was a tough play-by-the-rules guy who would not make a decision against his rules. He told me I would have to fly across the Andes mountains to Chile, spend the Sunday sightseeing, and locate the Argentinian Embassy on Monday to obtain an entry visa. After that, I could fly back to Buenos Aires.

Luckily, American Airlines was kind enough to cover the cost of my adjusted flights and hotel accommodations in Chile. Unluckily, I had no luggage with me, just my overnight bag, my lecture notes, and racquets.

Monday morning, I took care of all I had to do to return to Buenos Aires and boarded the return flight. I was extremely happy to see my host coach, Gustavo. He ushered me into his car, saying, "We have to move it since we have coaches arriving for your first lecture session in 45 minutes."

"How long a drive is it to the Asociacion Argentina de Tenis facility?" I asked.

About 30 minutes," he said. "It will be close!"

I felt okay. After all, I had my lecture notes and my racquets. I knew what I would present. I was ready to go, street clothes and all. *I can do this*, I kept telling myself.

We pulled into the facility parking lot. A bus pulled up alongside the car. I stared at the half-awake, tired-looking passengers that stumbled from the bus. "Who are these guys?" I asked.

"They are coaches from the north of Argentina who have traveled all night to participate in your clinics," he replied. I was moved. A whole new feeling of *I can do this* came over me.

My first session, in a large classroom, was on strokes. With a shade over 100 coaches seated in chairs, I noticed they had a difficult time seeing and hearing my presentation. So, I jumped onto a table to make my presentation more visible and audible. My head was just a few feet from the ceiling. I was making adjustments and dancing to present my material. I felt a mutual admiration between the coaches and me to pull off a great coaches workshop since everyone in the building was making sacrifices to make it happen. It went very well.

Following the session, many coaches came forward, holding my first tennis book that had been translated into Spanish for me to sign. The books looked well-used and dusty because the coaches taught their classes on clay courts, and their shoes, socks, and tennis books accumulated clay dust.

After such a hectic, unpredictable start to the workshop, things went very well. I got to wear my tennis clothes, which was enough to help me feel a lot better. The coaches enjoyed the sessions. The feedback was very positive.

It turned out to be a fabulous week with the best steaks in the world and outstanding shopping trips—particularly perusing Argentinian leather goods (shoes, bags, and other accessories). Gustavo and his staff did an outstanding job hosting me. I filed the trip under the successful column! However, I did put an asterisk under my signature and a note: Way to fight, Gundars!)

A SHORT STORY FROM A TRIP TO SINGAPORE

Over the years, I have had many memorable tennis assignments working as a speaker for the ITF. This is a short story from a trip to Singapore.

I spent a week in Singapore wearing a different hat each day, working with their top juniors, national men's and women's teams, physical education teachers, club tennis pros, and administrators, and running open clinics for the general public. It was a wide range of tennis-related events.

To help ensure a smooth-running week, I was assigned a coach from India to pick me up from my hotel and make sure I got to the right place on the right day at the right time.

For the first three days, we had lunch at three different, really great Indian restaurants. On the fourth day, my Indian host announced, "Today, we are going to a not-Indian restaurant for lunch." I remember thinking, *That works for me. Maybe a Chinese restaurant for a change.*

We arrived at the restaurant, which was yet another Indian restaurant. I said nothing as I really enjoy Indian food. Halfway through the meal, the waiter took some bread out from a nearby oven and brought it over to our table. My Indian host calmly said, "In South India, we have rice with our meals. In not-India, we have bread."

I got it!

MY MOST MEMORABLE SET OF TENNIS

My brother John was an outstanding dentist with a great personality and a second-to-none sense of humor. His athletic claim to fame was his javelin throwing.

In 1966, he competed in javelin for the University of Melbourne and, in that year, won the title as Australian Universities' Champion. Brother John was rock solid, 6'3," and could really toss that spear.

His tennis ability was just okay. As expected, his serving was monstrous, but he had little skill with his backhand. In short, he was a javelin thrower, and I was a tennis player. From time to time, we competed on the tennis court.

One example of his trickiness and sense of humor was as follows:

During one of our competitive sets of tennis, John was so desperate to beat me that he actually figured out a way to do it. He had a great first serve since serving is a natural throwing action similar to throwing a javelin. We were in the middle of a set, and I was up 5-2 with John serving, down 15-40. He ripped a first serve ace, then walked up to the net to shake hands. "I'm done," he said. "I hurt my shoulder and can't continue playing." (He kind of defaulted the set.)

When talking with his friends, John said, "Yeah, I aced my brother on the last point of the last game we played," giving listeners the impression he beat me.

I'd been up 5-2 and had a set point. Brotherly love and enjoyment of his sense of humor kept me from making an issue of his claim.

Too funny!

MOST UNUSUAL PRESENTATION

My most unusual presentation took place in the mid-1980s at the USTA National Tennis Teachers Conference held at the Roosevelt Hotel in New York City.

The conference was well attended by a couple of hundred coaches. The coaches were seated courtside and at an upstairs balcony that surrounded the court. I presented a session on "improvisation." My then 12-year-old daughter, Amy, helped demonstrate. The talk went well—innovative material and an entertaining presentation. The attendees' feedback was very complimentary. I came off the court, gave my daughter a hug, and whispered in her ear, "Well done! The coaches enjoyed the session."

Immediately following the presentation, Eve Kraft, the conference director, approached me with a serious facial expression, shook her head, and painfully whispered that the sound system for recording my session had broken down and there was no audio copy of my session. She wanted to know if I could repeat my session the next day. They had a gap in the program from 1-2 pm. The difference would be that no one would be watching! Without hesitation, both Amy and I said, "Sure!"

The re-do went even better than the original. Both father and daughter were more relaxed. The only part lacking was that we didn't have anyone to laugh at our jokes!

Eve Kraft was so appreciative of our "no hesitation" and "happy to re-do the session" attitude that she handed us front-row seats in the President's Box at the US Open for two nights. Amy also got a couple of pink US Open Women's T-shirts.

INTRODUCING PLAYERS WITH THEIR WINNING RECORDS

It has been a tradition for me to be the announcer, scorekeeper, and umpire for the annual Men's Doubles exhibition match at The Racquet Club in Portland, Oregon.

Over the past 20 years, many big names in the tennis world have played in the exhibition. The quality of play has been exceptional. Here are some of the players:

Patrick Galbraith

USTA President (2018-). Ranked #1 in the world in 1993 for Men's Doubles. Mixed Doubles champion at the US Open in 1994 and 1996.

Jonathan Stark

Ranked #1 in the world in Men's Doubles in 1994. Teamed with Byron Black in 1994 to win the French Open's Men's Doubles title. Won the Wimbledon Mixed Doubles title with Martina Navratilova in 1995.

Travis Parrott

Winner of the US Open Mixed Doubles in 2009.

Mike Tammen

Director of Tennis at The Racquet Club (2004-2021). Represented the United States in the World Seniors Competition for 16 years, competing in the 35-60 age groups, winning seven world titles over that 16-year period. Captained the Senior Davis Cup teams for the 50s, 55s, and 60s.

Brian Joelson

Former Grand Slam competitor. Won nine USTA National Father/Son titles with son Brett.

Eric Pickard

Perhaps the most impressive player I've had the pleasure of introducing at the annual doubles exhibition. He's a former coach at both the Multnomah Athletic Club and The Racquet Club in Portland, Oregon. He was an excellent teacher and an outstanding collegiate player. He tells the story of how honored he was to give playing lessons to legendary movie actor Harrison Ford whenever he came to Portland. Ford liked to spar and play out points during his lessons. Eric won most of their competitive play. Eric can claim a winning record against Harrison, and by association, indirect wins over Hans Solo and Indiana Jones. Are you kidding me? No!

From left to right:

Gundars Tilmanis, Travis Parrott, Mike Tammen, Jonathan Stark, Brian Joelson

AN EXERCISE IN MAKING ADJUSTMENTS AND STAYING UNDER CONTROL

This is a story from a trip to Paraguay in the mid-1980s. The ITF invited me to represent them and run a week-long tennis course for Paraguay's tennis coaches to be held in their capital city, Asuncion.

I did a little research to get a picture of where I was heading. I found out that Paraguay was a landlocked country right in the middle of South America, between Argentina, Brazil, and Bolivia. When ordering my airline tickets for the flight to Asuncion, I realized the flight from Portland to Florida to the middle of South America would be an all-day flight. I thought about my comfort during this all-day adventure and decided to wear a cozy warmup, thick woolly socks, and sandals. Then, on arrival in Asuncion, I'd head for the hotel to shower and dress nicely to meet my Paraguayan host tennis officials.

I was right that the flight and the lengthy layover in Florida made for a very long 24 hours. I arrived with a relieved, tired body but a happy disposition, ready to commence my tennis session with the Paraguayan coaches. Immediately upon exiting the plane, I started looking for a person holding a "Tilmanis" sign. To my surprise, three well-dressed gentlemen wearing suits and ties approached me. "Coach Tilmanis, welcome to Paraguay," they said, shaking my hand and gesturing for me to walk toward what looked like a private room at the airport.

On entering the room, I quickly noticed a few more well-dressed tennis officials and a rather large TV camera that looked interview-ready. There I was with my warmups, white socks, and sandals in the middle of one of the most exclusive, important, well-orchestrated events the Paraguay Tennis Association had ever held. It was a major event for them. My plan of heading to the hotel to freshen up, dress nicely, and meet the hosts had been thwarted.

I can remember feeling a bit embarrassed and a little awkward. I kept telling myself, *Be calm, keep smiling; you can survive this!* The tennis association had set up a beautiful, thoughtful, welcoming ceremony for me. I had to respond with my words and gestures as I had only a muted response with my attire! A moving Paraguayan flag-raising ceremony ensued, and a number of welcome speeches followed.

The TV interview felt more comfortable for me as I thanked the association for the warm welcome and outlined my program for the week. I had to dance and joke a little to tactfully get around a few of the tougher questions. For example, "Paraguay is playing Uruguay next month in the Davis Cup. How do you think we'll do?" I tried to think of the players involved in the Davis Cup and could not think of any of the players involved. I remember telling myself, *Stay calm, relax; you can survive*. I finally answered after realizing that I was in Paraguay. I responded, "I think it will be a close match, but I think Paraguay will win. Next question, please."

In short, I was deeply honored and impressed by the warm welcome I received from the Paraguay Tennis Association. I looked forward to the week. The coach that was assigned to pick me up at my hotel each morning and transport me to the various venues where I was speaking or demonstrating spoke no English, and I only spoke a few words of Spanish. Needless to say, we had to work extra hard with hand gestures, facial expressions, and diagrams scratched out on pieces of paper or restaurant menus to keep moving ahead. My host coach was a very happy fellow who did a lot of smiling and laughing, and it was all I could do to figure out what was coming next.

Between lectures and demonstration sessions, my host coach was adamant about showing me every corner of Asuncion. When he learned that I grew up in Australia, he engaged in an unrelenting mission of getting me to their local zoo to see the one kangaroo they had. He talked me into going. It was a hot, humid afternoon at the zoo. I can still remember the torturous conditions we endured—hundreds, no thousands, no millions, of mosquitoes constantly landing on our exposed skin. There was no way I was going to show any agitation or signs of being unhappy to be at the zoo. My host coach was just the nicest, most conscientious person imaginable. I toughed it out.

The on-court sessions (singles and doubles strategies, developing strokes, improvisation, anticipation, etc.) went very well. I had a great interpreter and knew my words of wisdom were getting through to the coaches because they laughed loudly when my jokes were translated. I knew that education was taking place. I was happy.

The on-court facility where the sessions were held had a protective roof to keep the sun off the courts, but the sides were wide open, so there was a continuous glare visible when playing. In short, it was a little tough to see. I had four coaches demonstrating a doubles overhead drill that involved some aggressive overhead hitting when low and behold, I was hit by an overhead ball and knocked unconscious. In the compromised glaring light conditions, I never saw the ball coming. I knew I was going down, so I quickly sat down and was out like a light.

When I woke up and opened my eyes, I looked around and couldn't remember where I was, just like in the comic books I read as a kid, when the hero was knocked out, only to wake up and say, "Where am I?" It took a while to remember where I was and what I was doing. I felt a wet, cold towel rolled around my neck and noticed

I was surrounded by a dozen coaches. They thought they had killed me! I was nauseous and just sat there, slowly looking around. I asked, "How long was I out for?" They told me I'd been out for about five minutes.

The week ended with an emotional thank you from the Tennis Association and an appreciative speech from me for the friendship and great hospitality. I told the group that I thoroughly enjoyed my week except for about five minutes of it. They laughed and emotionally conveyed, *All's well that ends well.*

I filed the week under the successful column.

WHO ARE YOU PLAYING FOR?

In the winter of 1990, I was teaching a private lesson to an aspiring young junior on an indoor court in Portland, Oregon.

It was one of those lessons where the student was dogging it—no footwork, no hustle, and no energy. He was wasting his time and mine. I was just beginning to think through how to deliver a verbal smack and get him motivated to play when a man in a suit and tie came up to the courtside window to watch. I stopped feeding him balls and motioned to the player to meet me at the net.

"I can't believe he's here," I whispered quietly to my student, then quickly returned to my teaching basket to continue the lesson. My student took a long, hard look at the gentleman in the window before returning to his baseline. The drill continued, and, yes, you can easily guess what happened. My student's energy level picked up; he chased every ball. He was back!

After the workout, he eagerly wanted to know who the gentleman was, hoping he was a racquet company representative or a USTA national coach.

"I have no idea who that was," I said. "For all I know, it could have been the soft drink man delivering to the snack bar." And then I let him have it. In a loud but controlled voice, I said, "If it takes a stranger watching your lesson to get you to play your most energized tennis, then you are not going to make it. You were playing for him. You have to play for yourself."

Every time you walk out onto a tennis court—whether for lessons, practice, practice matches, or tournament matches—you should get energized, excited to play and push the go button because you *are* playing for someone very important—*yourself.*

MIKE AND BOB BRYAN'S WONDERFUL GESTURE

In 2013, I started coaching twin boys Connor and Spencer Barnett. They developed into a very successful doubles team and were 6A High School State finalists in their last two years of high school. They started tennis competition as a serious doubles team as 11-year-olds and received a terrific motivational boost from the best legendary doubles team ever: the Bryan brothers!

The "boost" story starts when Connor and Spencer, as 11-year-olds, decided to trick-or-treat on Halloween as the Bryan brothers. Connor wore a white hat with the name "Bob" on it. Spencer had a hat with "Mike" on it. Armed with their racquets, they toured the neighborhood, each holding a sign:

Connor's sign: Doubles? You bring your brother. I'll bring mine!

Spencer's sign: The Bryan Brothers, Best Doubles Team in the History of Tennis.

As a co-speaker at various tennis conferences, I had befriended the

Bryan brothers' coach—their father, Wayne—and thought he would appreciate and enjoy seeing a photo of the Barnett boys and their Halloween costumes going as his sons. A few weeks after sending him the photos, I received a poster from him of his boys, Mike and Bob. The poster was signed to Connor and Spencer with the inscription: "Twins Rule!"

This was a heartwarming story of gratitude, appreciation, motivation, inspiration, and kindness from both sets of twins!

A TENNIS PROGRAM THAT INCLUDED THE WHOLE FAMILY

In March of 1988, I received an invitation from Professor John Bloomfield, Chairman of the Australian Institute of Sport, to spend a month in Western Australia as the Bicentennial Alcoa Tennis Coach in Residence. It was an honor to be selected to help the Australian tennis community celebrate their bicentennial. (It was a double pleasure for me since, while I now reside with my family in America, it was Australia where I was introduced to tennis and learned to play and love the sport.)

My mission was to present a variety of tennis-related programs for a wide audience:

- Tennis teachers at the club, high school, and university levels
- Tennis administrators at the club and state levels
- The junior and senior state tennis teams
- The parents of junior tennis players
- The general public - that is, any tennis enthusiast In short, I was to wear a variety of presentation hats.

The bicentennial tennis assignment was a kind of homecoming for me. Having grown up in Melbourne, my parents, brother, and other relatives were all still living in the Land Down Under. However, our four daughters were born in the USA and were most excited about the possibility of joining me on this adventure, particularly to see their grandparents, relatives, and a koala!

My actual birthplace was Riga, Latvia, so when feeling a little "cheeky" or mischievous on giving these presentations, I would begin as follows: "As President of the Latvian, Australian American Tennis Coaches Association, I would like to thank you all for coming to my session this morning." (Then, I could enjoy imagining their realization that if there even was such an organization, there couldn't possibly be many members!)

The Tilmanis family did travel, all six of us, to Australia for this wonderful event. It was quite an undertaking to move our group around from one continent to another, and I felt people eyeballing us as we strode through the various airports. What other travelers would have seen was a father, followed by a mother, followed by four young girls ranging in age from three to thirteen. I could just imagine passengers' thoughts as we headed toward the boarding gates. *Poor guy! One wife and four daughters. He probably has a tough time getting into the bathroom when at home!* We took a family photo of the four girls at the Portland Airport as we embarked on this adventure, quite intentionally under the "Made in Oregon" shop sign, enjoying the humor of the truth of it!

Some Trip Highlights

Daughter Amy was already an accomplished tennis player and was annually ranked in the top five players of her age group in the USTA Northwest Region. She became a valuable assistant, regularly helping me set up, demonstrate, and tidy up after sessions at the various tennis events and venues.

We shared some exciting moments during our travels around the state of Western Australia, one being an attempted early morning ocean swim in the township of Fremantle. This is just a short distance south of Perth, which is Western Australia's capital city. We wasted no time when we hit the beach and raced to dive into the water. Just as quickly as we entered, we exited and regrouped back on land. "Oh my gosh!" yelled Amy. "I can't believe all those jellyfish!" So much for our early morning swimming workout.

Australia is famous for a huge variety of wildlife, many species only found in Australia and many of which are poisonous. We did not wait to find out if these jellyfish were dangerous but decided to adjust our workout to a half-mile jog along the beach.

On many occasions, whenever possible, actually, the whole family sought out the wildlife sanctuaries. There are so many animals and plants indigenous only to Australia. We viewed kangaroos, koalas, kookaburras, platypuses, emus, cockatoos, and snakes. Special moments were feeding kangaroos, being up right next to an emu when they emit their signature rumbling, drum-like noise, searching for the koalas perched up comfortably in the nooks of eucalyptus branches, visiting with and listening to the "talking" cockatoos. There were train rides with an overview of the park and trails leading right alongside many animal enclosures for up close and personal views!

Anyone who knows the Oregon beach waters will know how incredibly cold they are. Perth's Mediterranean climate allows for swimming in the ocean year-round. It was such a treat for the whole family to also visit the beaches of Western Australia as the water was swimmable, and there were seashells galore of all shapes and sizes from such an assortment of species. The coast of Oregon is so rocky that shells don't find their way to the sand in one piece often. Here, there were shell treasures everywhere!

Family reconnecting was also a super bonus of this Australian trip. The girls visiting with their grandparents from the Latvian-Australian side, seeing my brother John and his growing family, and letting my girls meet their cousins and relatives—or "re-los" as the Aussies love to shorten it to—were incalculable highlights. This brings up the topic of learning a new language. The Aussies do like to shortcut many words:

- Postman = "postie"
- University = "uni"
- Breakfast = "breaky"
- Watching television = watching the "telly"

Another Aussie language learning experience was finding their delightfully different terms for some of our familiar words like:

- Popsicles = "icy poles"
- Sidewalks = "footpaths"
- Cotton Candy = "fairy floss"
- Afternoon = "arvo" as in "See you this arvo!"
- If things are not going well, things are "crook."
- If you want to pay for a meal for the group, you say, "I'll shout."
- And, of course, dinner is called "tea" and doesn't mean just a "cuppa."

The Aussies are the masters of running words together as they apply the Aussie drawl to the English language in what is called "speaking Strine."

- What are you doing? = "Watchadoing?"
- How is it going? = "Owsitgoing?"
- Mind your own business = "Mindjaownbusiness! "
- And one of my personal favorites, which turns "Did you have a good week-end?" Into "Javagoodweegend?"

After mailing off a letter of gratitude to the Australian Institute of Sport for the opportunity to be part of their bicentennial celebration, there was time to reflect on the experience. The evaluations and feedback were positive, and it felt terrific to contribute on so many levels. We were able to meet with coaches, parents, recreational and competitive players, young players, and adult players. It was rewarding to give a bit back to the sport that has given so much to me. My wife, Janet, and our four daughters, still talk of the fabulous trip to Australia to this day. I have filed it away in the all-around successful column.

MY MOST HEARTWARMING AND EMOTIONAL TENNIS COACHES WORKSHOP

Latvian Tennis Federation Coaches Workshop

June 27-28, 2004

Riga, Latvia

First, a little historical background: I was born in Riga, Latvia, in 1944 on June 6. Yes, the very same day that the Allied Forces landed in Normandy during WWII, called D- Day. My mother had her own D—for disaster—the day I was born.

After the conclusion of WWII, my parents, my younger brother, John, and I became refugees, and my parents had to choose from a couple of countries where to immigrate. They chose Australia.

We arrived in Melbourne, Australia, in 1948. No one in our family could speak English at that time, so, needless to say, it was a very trying, tough transition.

My first day of school was a recorded testament to that. An article in the local Melbourne newspaper was titled "The Screamer." It read: "Yarra Park State School proudly boasted of a record today. Of all the newcomers, only one screamed, a five-year-old whose range was shattering. But he was soon quieted by Mrs. A.M. McPherson, who is a specialist in soothing the preliminary fears of five-year-olds. Five-year-old Gundars Tilmanis from Latvia, who cannot speak a word of English, is one of about a dozen new Australian children at Yarra Park School. New Australian parents like to send their children to Yarra Park because they themselves have English language lessons there twice weekly."

So, 54 years after my screaming episode, with mixed emotions, I had an invitation to return to Riga, Latvia.

During those 54 years, I had earned a Master of Science in Physical Education from the University of Oregon, had coached tennis in both the collegiate and tennis club settings for 38 years, was an active member of the USTA, USPTA, and PTR organizations, and had participated in programs for the International Tennis Federation.

The Invitation to Return to Latvia to Coach the Coaches

In January 2003, I gave two presentations at the Australian Tennis Coaches Conference (held in conjunction with the Australian Open Grand Slam Tennis Tournament). Following one of my presentations, I was approached by an attendee who extended his hand, shook mine, and said, "Good job." Then, he introduced himself as Valdis Libietis, a Latvian tennis coach and administrator. He continued talking. "You are Latvian, right?" I replied, "Yes." Next came the invitation: "Would you like to come to Latvia to conduct a workshop for our Latvian tennis coaches?"

There was a speechless pause. I got a little emotional. After having to leave my birthplace 54 years ago, I not only had an invitation to return but an opportunity to contribute to the development of tennis in Latvia. I replied with an emphatic "Yes," again and said, "I would love to do that!" At the time, in 2004, I was living and teaching tennis in Portland, Oregon.

The Latvian Tennis Federation Coaches Workshop was set for June 27-29, 2004. My wife, Janet, and youngest daughters, Kelly and Casey, joined me on the flight from Portland, Oregon, to Riga. Then, my father arranged to join us and flew to Riga from Australia. I felt extra comfortable with the trip as a family affair.

We landed in Riga on Friday, June 25, 2004. The coaches workshop was set to start at 8:30 am on Sunday, June 27, so we had plenty of time to settle in. Greeting us at the airport were Valdis Libietis, officials from the Latvian Tennis Federation, and a number of family relatives that had remained in Riga at the end of WWII.

We experienced the Latvia tradition of receiving welcoming flowers—so many flowers that our family of four could not hold them comfortably to take them to our waiting transportation. Our hosts helped us out. It was the warmest welcome I had ever experienced.

The coaches workshop was held at a facility in a town on the coast called Lielupe, about 45 minutes by train or car from Riga. They had indoor and outdoor tennis courts and an elegant wooden stadium that comfortably seated 4,000-5,000 spectators. All of this surrounded by a robust, healthy-looking pine forest. A beautiful setting!

The night before the workshop, Valdis asked if I would feel more comfortable speaking in English, and he would translate into Russian. He thought there might be some White Russians or Polish coaches registered. All the Latvian coaches could speak Russian, and I said, "Sounds good."

Then about a half-hour before the first workshop session, I noticed 45 coaches had gathered. I asked Valdis where the coaches were from. He said that they were all Latvian. Of the 90 or so total Latvian coaches, half of them were there! I made a quick decision to present in Latvian since my Latvian was pretty good. I asked Valdis to help me out if I needed it.

It was a good decision. I got the terminology down fairly quickly. For example, I would say, "Hit the ball into the open court." The Latvian coaches would call it the "free" court.

The sessions went very smoothly. There were two to three young Latvian coaches who spoke English very well and helped me out by correcting my Latvian a few times.

Then there was ample off time for my father to show me around Riga. "See that four-story building on the other side of the road? You were born on the third floor. The bridge we are coming to is where your mother and I would meet between classes."

I experienced many exciting, nostalgic moments and enjoyed meeting with relatives. My parents had retained many of their Latvian traditions, customs, and foods, which I had experienced regularly while growing up, and I was very pleased to actually get to enjoy some of these food specialties in Riga, like:

- Latvian Ryebread (second to none!)
- Potato pancakes
- Sauerkraut
- Piragi
- Fresh salads with dill

Without a doubt, being able to revisit my homeland made this my most heartwarming, emotionally rewarding tennis event ever!

LATVIAN TENNIS FEDERATION
COACHES WORKSHOPS
JUNE 27 – 29, 2004

Date	Time	Activity
Sunday, June 27, 2004	8:30 am	Opening Introductions
	9 – 10:30 am	Session 1 • Drills that handle many players on one court • How one coach can handle 2 – 3 courts at a time
	10:45 am – 12:15 pm	Session 2 • Preparing your players for competition (one coach, one player)
	12:15 – 1:30 pm	Lunch (on your own)
	1:30 – 3 pm	Session 3 • Teaching tennis skills • Question and answer session
	3:15 – 4:30 pm	Session 4 • Shot selection • Improvisation
Monday, June 28, 2004	9 – 10:30 am	Session 5 • Teaching singles strategies
	10:45 am – 12:15 pm	Session 6 • Preparing your players for competition (one coach, two players)
	12:15 – 1:30 pm	Lunch (on your own)
	1:30 – 3 pm	Session 7 • Doubles strategies and drills
	3:15 – 4:30 pm	Session 8 • The Mental Game ("Keep your head – don't lose it.")

Tuesday, June 29, 2004	9 – 10:30 am	Session 9 • Preparing your players for competition (one coach, 4 – 6 players)
	10:45 am – 12:15 pm	Session 10 • Anticipation • Question and answer session
	12:15 – 1:30 pm	Lunch (on your own)
	1:30 – 3 pm	Session 11 • Playing on clay courts
	3:15 – 4:30 pm	Session 12 • Fun group drills for competitive players
	4:30 – 4:45 pm	Workshop Closes

All sessions are on court except session 8.

2012 USTA TENNIS TEACHERS CONFERENCE FACULTY EMERITUS AWARD

When Kirk Anderson called me in mid-June of 2012 and informed me of my selection for the subject award, I thought to myself, *This has to be a mistake. Old people get emeritus awards, and I'm not an old person…or am I?*

After doing some thinking, I realized I first started speaking at the USTA Tennis Teachers Conference in 1975, and now it's 2012. Did I really speak regularly for 37 years? Perhaps over 30 times?! I guess so! So, I must be an "old person" and, therefore, totally deserving of the award.

The conference was the highlight of my year. It was always so well run, and the program included outstanding speakers. I was grateful that the USTA had given me so many speaking opportunities to share my ideas and, in turn, interact with conferees and listen to other speakers. It was exciting to be surrounded by highly motivated tennis coaches. We helped each other become better teachers, administrators, and promoters of the sport we all loved.

I was honored and happy to receive the 2012 USTA Tennis Teachers Conference Faculty Emeritus Award.

The photograph of the awards ceremony shows David Haggerty on the left, Kirk Anderson on the right, and me in the middle. David was the 2012 USTA President and has been the ITF President since 2015. Kirk Anderson was the 2012 Director of the USTA Tennis Teachers Conference.

The USTA Tennis Teachers Conference Emeritus Award recognizes an individual who has made a significant and long-term contribution as a speaker at the annual USTA Tennis Teachers Conference. The award says: "An internationally recognized tennis teacher, Gundars 'Til' Tilmanis has authored three instructional books. He combines his science background with years of teaching privately and coaching college teams.

Tilmanis is known for translating theory into a practical system of player development. A regular speaker at the Tennis Teachers Conference since 1975, he earned a Masters in Physical Education at the University of Oregon."

From left to right:
David Haggerty, Gundars Tilmanis, Kirk Anderson

About The Author

Gundars Tilmanis ("Til") is an internationally recognized tennis coach, author, and lecturer. He graduated from the University of Oregon with a Masters's Degree in Physical Education. Til is generally regarded as one of the top teaching clinicians in the world today. Known for his quick wit and extensive teaching background he has worked for many years as a clinician for both the United States Tennis Association (USTA) and the International Tennis Federation (ITF). He has spoken repeatedly at the USTA Tennis Teachers Conference in New York, the PTR International Symposium and the USPTA National Convention. He has delivered a broad range of tennis related lectures to audiences throughout the world. During the past 30 years he has lectured throughout the United States, Japan, Latvia, Guatemala, Spain Singapore Paraguay, Argentina, Canada, and Australia.

His innovative energetic style of coaching has drawn praise throughout the tennis world.

Born in Riga, Latvia, raised in Melbourne Australia, Til currently resides in Portland OR in the USA and consultant teaches privately.

Made in United States
Troutdale, OR
12/31/2023

16573265R00120